RECLAIMING ADOPTION

Missional Living through the Rediscovery of Abba Father

Dan Cruver, Editor
John Piper | Richard D. Phillips
Scotty Smith | Jason Kovacs

Cruciform Press | Released January, 2011

To my son Daniel, who through his three years of
unrelenting suffering and his untimely death taught
me not merely how to care for the weak and
vulnerable, but how to care for others in and through
my own weakness. Together, my son Daniel and
I eagerly await our adoption as sons, that is, the
redemption of our bodies (Romans 8:23).
-Dan Cruver

CruciformPress

© 2011 by Dan Cruver. All rights reserved.
CruciformPress.com | info@CruciformPress.com

"Jesus protects the fatherless and the widow. And Jesus isn't dead anymore. The Spirit of Christ is afoot in the churches of the Lord Jesus all over the world, pulling us into Jesus' mission for the orphan, the stranger, the marginalized. This book is part of that pull. The authors writing here are some of the most fearless thinkers and activists in the Christian orphan care movement. Read. Be empowered. And then join Jesus for the orphans of the world."

Russell D. Moore, Author of *Adopted for Life*

"There is no greater need in our day than theological clarity. We live in a pragmatic, hype-driven, emotionally manipulated spiritual landscape. We need the ancient wisdom of the Bible, not another business book or glory story from some cool church. Dan has brought us near to the heart of God, who by His Spirit cries out in our hearts, 'Abba, Father.' As you read this book, you will sense the need to embrace your own acceptance as God's adopted child."

Darrin Patrick, Author of *Church Planter*

"*Reclaiming Adoption* captures the heart and soul of what it means to be a child of God, walk as the feet of Jesus on this earth, and live for eternity with our loving Savior. Make no mistake, this isn't simply a book on adoption. It's about the reason we were created and how we are to spend the rest of our days loving others."

Tom Davis, Author of *Fields of the Fatherless*

"*Reclaiming Adoption* is the best kind of theological work: it sings and it sends! As I read, I wanted to praise the Triune God for his great love. Then I felt the urgency of the call to live that love among the world's orphans. Completely accessible, *Reclaiming Adoption* is thoroughly grounded in Scripture and flows from the great heart of the Church's historic understanding of the Word. The authors have uncovered new depths and fresh passion in expressing how adoption clarifies the meaning of our union with Christ. *Reclaiming Adoption* expands our vision to the fuller glory of the whole narrative of Christ's work. Thus, this book can transform the worship, education, and mission of any church bold enough to explore its truth."

Gerrit Dawson, Author of *Called by a New Name*

"A stirring call to be involved in the ministry of adoption for Jesus' sake. Gospel-centered. Prophetic. Practical. *Reclaiming Adoption* addresses an issue that has transformed our church as much as any other."

J.D. Greear, Lead Pastor, The Summit Church, Durham, NC

"Many Christians today would not invest much time toward thinking about adopting an orphan. It is not unrelated that the doctrine of adoption is sadly one of the most overlooked doctrines amongst Christians today. It is into this void that *Reclaiming Adoption* speaks so powerfully and reclaims the central place that adoption must take in the thinking of any child of God. *Reclaiming Adoption* is a must read; it will tell your head who you are and move your heart to live in response."

Steve Chong, Director, Rice movement, Sydney, Australia

"I am grateful for the work that Dan has done to lift our eyes to the grand story of adoption. With spiritual insight and effective teaching, *Reclaiming Adoption* will help believers better understand our place with Christ and work in His kingdom."

Ed Stetzer, President, LifeWay Research

"I can't recall ever hearing about, much less reading, a book like this before. Simply put, this remarkable volume fills a much-needed gap in our understanding of what the Bible says both about God's adoption of us and our adoption of others. I highly recommend it."

Sam Storms, Author of *The Singing God: Discover the Joy of Being Enjoyed by God*

"If you want your church to be a church for the great commission and for the orphan, reading *Reclaiming Adoption* is where you need to start."

Matt Carter, Lead Pastor, The Austin Stone Community Church

"The wonderful good news of our adoption by God is such an important truth for Christians today. Too many of us live as slaves, distanced from God because we do not embrace him as our loving Father. As a result our obedience is reduced to mere duty instead of being animated by joy. How can we put this right? This book is a great place to start. Enriching theology and missional application are beautifully interwoven. The result is a book that will warm your heart and might just change your life."

Tim Chester, Author of *You Can Change* and *Total Church*

"*Reclaiming Adoption* consistently reminds the evangelical orphan care movement that it always must be the love of Christ that compels us. Any lesser motivation will ultimately run dry. It is the gospel alone that can carry us forward to 'defend the fatherless' through adoption, foster care, and orphan care across the globe."

Jedd Medefind, President, Christian Alliance for Orphans

Table of Contents

CruciformPress.com

Published by Cruciform Press, Adelphi, Maryland | info@CruciformPress.com |
Copyright © 2011 by Dan Cruver, All rights reserved. | ISBN: 978-1-4564595-0-5 |
Unless otherwise indicated, all Scripture quotations are taken from: The Holy Bible:
English Standard Version, Copyright © 2001 by Crossway Bibles, a division of Good
News Publishers. Used by permission. All rights reserved. | Italics or bold text within
Scripture quotations indicates emphasis added.

One
ADOPTION OF THE PRODIGALS

Dan Cruver

One of my dreams is that when Christians hear the word *adoption*, they will think first about their adoption by God. I am far from alone in this dream. I share it with the co-authors of this book, with those who have attended *Together for Adoption* conferences, and with innumerable other Christians, beginning with the Apostle Paul.

The word *adoption* is rooted in an ancient Greco-Roman legal practice, and until Paul everyone understood it as referring to human adoption, what we might also call *horizontal* adoption. But Paul gave the concept a theological underpinning by grounding it in *vertical* adoption—God's adoption of sinners. Paul knew something that much of the Church today seems unaware of—if we learn to first think vertically about adoption, and only then horizontally, we will enjoy deeper communion with the triune God *and* experience greater missional engagement with the pain and suffering of this world. That's what this book is about. We believe:

- the doctrine of adoption has been widely neglected within the Church historically;
- it remains neglected within much of the evangelical church today;
- a proper theological grounding of horizontal adoption *within* vertical adoption has profound implications for our understanding of both aspects, and therefore;
- to the extent we can recapture theological balance regarding adoption, the Church will be transformed and our witness to the world will be radically redefined.

Why is the theology of adoption so neglected? It's a matter of where Christians have put their attention. It is generally believed that the Church has created thousands of creeds and confessions, with more than 150 being created during the Reformation period alone. Yet in scouring almost 1,900 years of Church history, Philip Schaff found only six creeds that contain a section on theological adoption.

To be fair, there are some good reasons for this. The early Church was primarily concerned with defining and defending the doctrines of Christ and the Trinity. Similarly, the Reformation and post-Reformation Church focused largely on defending the doctrine of justification. We can be eternally glad and grateful these battles were resolutely fought and won. At the same time, the tight focus on a relatively small number of doctrines unintentionally prevented the Church from developing thorough scriptural teaching on vertical adoption.

This is largely why Christians tend to interpret the word *adoption* first (and often only) in terms of adopting children. This is also why vertical adoption is not on the Christian community's radar to the extent it ought to be; why God's Fatherhood and our status as his beloved children are not a regular part of our vocabulary; and why the Church's missional engagement in the world is not informed and shaped—to the extent it can and should be—by Scripture's teaching on our adoption by God. Our prayer is that this book will contribute to changing all that, for God's glory and our good.

Our Prodigal Race

Few stories have the ability to pierce us as deeply as Jesus' Parable of the Prodigal Son from Luke 15:11-32 (I suggest you read the passage now unless you are already very familiar with it). In recent years, Tim Keller's teaching on this parable has served the Church well by rightly focusing our attention on the father and his relationship, not merely with the younger son, but also with the older son.[1] As Jesus makes clear at the start, this parable is about both sons, and both are estranged from their father.

The younger son manifests his estrangement by breaking the rules, and the older son manifests his by keeping them. The older son may have been "on mission" with the father *externally*—doing what he was "supposed" to do—but he certainly wasn't on mission with him *internally*. His heart was not aligned missionally with the heart of the father. Once it became clear to him that the father dealt with his sons according to grace and not according to merit, his emotional capital and missional commitment evaporated. No longer was he capable of "serving" the father. Nor did he have any interest in aligning himself with the father's agenda of welcoming home lost sons. Thus, *both* sons are prodigals, neither one living in loving communion with the father.

Deep underneath the differing externals of these two sons' behaviors is the fact that both were "sons of disobedience" and "children of wrath" (Ephesians 2:2-3). But the beauty and wonder of the Parable of the Prodigal Son(s) is that it puts the father's love on display—a love that embraces the younger son with uninhibited joy (Luke 15:20) and goes out to entreat the older to come join the celebration (v. 28). In both cases, the father comes to the rebels to bring them into *his* joy, his *home*. This father loves prodigals.

We are the prodigals whom Jesus, the true and eternal Son, came to bring home. Some of us are more like the younger brother, and some the older. Look closely enough, however, and most of us from time to time can resemble either one.

All of us were created in the image of God so that we could participate in the communion of love between the Father and the Son (as we will explore at various points in this book), but we were cut off from that communion because of our sin and rebellion. We became an entire prodigal race, sons of disobedience and children of wrath. As a result, all of us have what C.S. Lewis calls a "longing to be reunited with something in the universe from which we now feel cut off, to be on the inside of some door which we have always only seen from the outside."[2]

The door that seems so impenetrable is the eternal communion of love between the Father and the Son. The story of the Bible is that God the Father sent his only true and eternal Son on a mission, and that mission was to bring many wayward and rebellious sons home to glory (Hebrews 2:10). *That* is the Story behind the story of the Prodigal Sons. That is the only story that gives our stories any meaning or significance.

The Story of Adoption

If we consider the Parable of the Prodigal Sons within the larger context of Scripture, we find that it is really the story of adoption—the adoption of humanity as a prodigal race (Genesis 3:6). Maybe you are thinking, *Jesus' parable in Luke 15 can't be about adoption. The two brothers were already the father's sons; they were just estranged. Adoption is for orphans, not sons.*

That would be a reasonable response, but a misguided one, because the logic starts from human adoption. It takes adoption as we understand it horizontally and tries to force the definition of vertical adoption into the same mold. Yes, the Apostle Paul borrowed the term *adoption* from the Greco-Roman horizontal practice, but he altered and expanded the word, filling it with rich redemptive-historical meaning. When Paul says *adoption*, he does *not* mean it the same way we usually do. We should not try to export the attributes of human adoption to divine adoption, because that is not what Paul was intending to communicate. Instead, we should import into our view of human adoption Scripture's teaching that those who are outside the Father are without hope or home. Let us allow Scripture to remold our concept of adoption, so we can take on a God-centered view rather than a man-centered one.

Paul is the only writer in Scripture to employ the term *adoption*, and he does so in four separate passages.[3] Looking at each passage in turn transports us to four crucial events in the grand story of redemption. Together, these events reveal the adoption of sinners to be God's ultimate purpose. They also have the power to completely overhaul our understanding of adoption.

Before Time: Ephesians 1:4-5 In this passage, Paul states that God the Father "chose us in him before the foundation of the world, that we should be holy and blameless before him. In love he predestined us for adoption as sons through Jesus Christ." Thus, we see that God's first work of adoption happened even before he created the universe. God did this, Paul emphasizes, "in love." Before the first molecule was formed, God marked us out with incomparable care—he predestined us—for the great privilege of being his beloved children through adoption. Adoption was not a divine afterthought. It was in God's triune mind and heart before the first tick of human history's clock. Adoption therefore predates the universe itself. Only God and his triune love are "bigger" than adoption.

Israel: Romans 9:4 Here, Paul identifies adoption as

one of the great privileges Israel enjoyed as God's chosen people: "They are Israelites, and to them belong *the adoption*, the glory, the covenants, the giving of the law, the worship, and the promises." Scholars believe that Israel received adoption—that is, officially became God's *corporate* son—when God declared them a nation at Mt. Sinai, three months *after* he delivered them from Egypt. Thus, God redeemed them *before* he adopted them. He redeemed them *in order* to adopt them.

Of course, Israel repeatedly failed in its sonship by rejecting the Father's love, replaying the story of Adam's rebellion. God's mission to bring many wayward and rebellious sons home to glory seemed doomed. Yet through Israel, God's corporate son through adoption, the eternal and perfect Son would be sent to redeem humanity, thereby preserving God's perfect plan.

Jesus: Galatians 4:4-6 "When the fullness of time had come, God sent forth his Son, born of woman, born under the law, to redeem those who were under the law, *so that we might receive adoption as sons.*" Here, Paul identifies adoption as the grand purpose or objective of redemption, and he could not have written it more clearly: "...*so that* we might receive adoption"! Once again, adoption shows up at a watershed moment within the unfolding story of redemption. Just as God redeemed Israel in order that he might adopt them, so also has God redeemed us in order that he might adopt us! Redemption is not the end of God's work. Adoption as sons is.

New Heavens & New Earth: Romans 8:15,22-23 Finally, adoption is central to the *end* of redemption's story. In verse 23, Paul writes, "And not only the creation, but we ourselves, who have the firstfruits of the Spirit, groan inwardly as we wait eagerly for *adoption as sons*, the redemption of our bodies." Paul identifies the glorification of our bodies as a final outward manifestation of our adoption. When the story of redemption reaches its intended goal, the Bible calls it "adoption." On that climactic day the heavens and the earth will be transformed into our Father's house. The renewed earth will become the place where we forever enjoy our Father's love as his sons and daughters. Paul's use of adoption in Romans 8 teaches us that missional living is not directionless living. Missional Christians daily fix their eyes on the climax of God's work of adoption—God's renewed heavens and earth.

So we see that Paul teaches that God does not merely redeem us—through adoption he brings us into the warmth, love, and gladness of his own family. Redemption was never intended to be God's "be-all and end-all" work of grace. God redeemed us *in his Son* so that he might love us and delight in us even as he loves and delights in his eternal Son. As we shall see, adoption is God's act of making room within his triune love for prodigals who are without hope, and providing them with homes in this world and the world to come. This is the story of adoption.

Now it is easier to see why the Parable of the Prodigal Sons is truly about adoption. From God's perspective, adoption is not essentially about orphans at all. It is essentially about estrangement. Adoption is about God taking into his home those who have rebelled against him. All humanity is naturally estranged from God. We are all rebels, all disobedient sons, for we are all made in his image and created to worship him, yet we have rejected him—as did Adam, as did Israel. Adoption is about the reconciliation of the rebellious. Our confusion comes when we look at human adoption and end up focusing on the fact that a child needs parents. God focuses on the fact that a lost person needs saving.

As we shall see later in this book, the *ultimate* purpose of human adoption by Christians, therefore, is not to give orphans parents, as important as that is. It is to place them in a Christian home that they might be positioned to receive the gospel, so that within that family, the world might witness a representation of God taking in and genuinely loving the helpless, the hopeless, and the despised.

Adoption and Mission

Today, God seems to be awakening his people to the importance of Scripture's teaching on this subject. The authors of this book are convinced that such an awakening will strengthen the Church's involvement in God's mission in the world. When Christians rediscover God's extravagant love for and delight in them, they begin to live differently. They begin to live missionally. Our goal here is not to define or explain the mission of God in any detail. We want to further equip you for sustained, joyful engagement and participation *in* that mission. These first four chapters, therefore, explore the interwoven stories behind God's work of adoption in the world and its implications for Christian mission. The chapters by Scotty Smith, Rick Phillips, Jason Kovacs, and John Piper then focus on various implications of adoption for missional living.

To live missionally means to live each waking moment in light of the gospel so that it increasingly affects every part of our lives for the glory of God's grace in our fallen world. Our hope for this book is that Scripture's teaching on adoption will better equip you to live daily in the good news of the gospel.

As believers, particularly in the West, it is easy for us to look at the decline of Christianity's cultural influence, the spread of a secular mindset, a volatile political climate globally, and our own internal struggles with sin, and conclude that the sky is falling. It's easy for us to look at the world and ourselves through the narrow lens of what's wrong with both, rather than through the wide-angle lens of what God has done, is doing, and will do in the world for his glory and our good. The narrow lens hinders Christian mission. The wide-angle mobilizes and serves it.

Making sure that we are looking at our world and ourselves through the proper lens is critical for Christian mission. I would contend that adoption is the proper lens through which to view the entire story of redemption.

Few things hinder action within the Christian life more than being unsure of God's love for us personally. Returning for a moment to the story of the prodigals, in *Children of the Living God*, Sinclair Ferguson sheds a particular kind of light on the prodigal son who left home. As he was returning to his father, the prodigal planned to say that he was no longer worthy to be called a son, which was certainly true. Convinced that, in the depth of his rebellion and rejection of the father, he had lost all hope of receiving the father's love, he intended to offer himself as a slave, hoping merely to survive. Little does the prodigal know, however, that his father eagerly awaits his return.

Ferguson sees something in the prodigal's thinking that parallels how we as Christians often think of God and his fatherly love for us:

> Jesus was underlining the fact that—despite assumptions to the contrary—the reality of the love of God for us is often the last thing in the world to dawn upon us. As we fix our eyes upon ourselves, our past failures, our present guilt, it seems impossible to us that the Father could love us. Many Christians go through much of their life with the prodigal's suspicion. Their concentration is upon their sin and failure; all their thoughts are introspective.[5]

When the prodigal son says, "I will arise and go to my father, and I will say to him, 'Father, I have sinned against heaven and before you. I am no longer worthy to be called your son. Treat me as one of your hired servants'" (Luke 15:18-19), he is thinking in terms of wages earned rather than extravagant love and grace received. It's as if he is thinking, "I ended up in the far country by squandering my father's wealth, so maybe I can *earn* my way back into his house."

When we as believers relate to God the Father as this prodigal son relates to his father, we are slow to return to

God after we sin. We don't anticipate—let alone expect—his fatherly embrace. And when we do return to him, we think of him primarily as our master and not our Father. As a result, real Christian joy is absent, passionate Christian living is lacking, and Christian mission is severely hindered.

Christians who doubt God's love for them will not mobilize for mission. Unless we know the Father delights in us even as he delights in Jesus, we will lack the emotional capital necessary to resist complacency and actively engage in missional living. The only people who can truly turn their eyes outward in mission are those who knowingly live within and enjoy the loving gaze of their heavenly Father.

I believe that a biblical understanding of God's Fatherhood will cause us to be better able to look outside ourselves in service to others. If we are not confident of his love, our eyes will turn inward, and our primary concerns will be *our* needs, *our* lack, *our* disappointment, rather than the needs of those around us. As a result, we'll be afraid to take risks or do the hard things even if they are necessary. Or we will do the externals of missional living as an attempt to earn God's acceptance or to keep him and our fellow-Christians off our backs. We will relate to him as if we are wage-earners rather than as his dearly beloved children, the ones in whom he delights.

The logic of wage-earning does not flow out of the of the gospel of grace. The gospel is joyful news because it speaks to us of the Father's love that has come to us freely in Jesus Christ.

Two
ADOPTION AND THE TRINITY

Dan Cruver

The Story behind both the Parable of the Prodigal
Sons and our story of adoption is the story of the triune[4]
God's mission in history to share his Trinitarian love
with us as his adopted sons. Given that we live between
the times—between our initial entrance into God's
family (Galatians 4:4-5) and the consummation of our
adoption at the redemption of our bodies (Romans
8:23)—we still battle daily with prodigal tendencies.
Hardly a day goes by that we are not tempted merely to
go on "mission" with the Father externally, doing what
we are "supposed" to do, without being on mission with
him internally. Like the prodigal sons in Luke 15, we are
daily tempted to exchange the *love* of the Father for the
things of the Father.

Our hearts all too often, as Tim Keller writes, long
for "a successful career, love, material possessions, even
family,"[6] instead of God. This is idolatry. An idol, Keller
continues, "is anything more important to you than God,

anything that absorbs your heart and imagination more than God, anything you seek to give you what only God can give."[7] But as the elder brother in Luke 15 shows us, our obedience to God can be an idol when it is more important to us than our relationship with God. In other words, we can easily exchange our enjoyment of God internally for our obedience to God externally. Whatever form it takes, our idolatry is therefore a daily threat to Christian faith and action. Although our obedience to God is meant to flow out of our enjoyment of God, living by faith is a daily challenge for us because we enter this world loving the things of the Father rather than the Father himself. Therefore, in order to maintain faithful, long-term engagement in missional living, it is essential that we deepen our understanding and experience of the Trinity, as well as the communion of love that the members of the Trinity enjoy with each other.

We were made *by* and *for* the triune God. Consequently, as Cornelius Plantinga writes, all of us "long for wholeness, for fulfillment, and for the final good that believers call God," whether we realize it or not. But idolatry, Plantinga continues, "taps this vital spiritual force and draws off its energies to objects and processes that drain [us] instead of filling [us]. Accordingly, [we long] not for God but for transcendence, not for joy but only for pleasure—and sometimes for mere escape from pain."[8] This perversion of our longing for God can have its fingerprints all over our hearts as well as our missional engagement in the world. Idolatry is not a respecter of prodigals or of elder brothers. With unbelievable ease, idolatry infects both religious and irreligious hearts.

This is why the story of our adoption is such good news. One way to look at adoption is to see it as God's work to free us from the insanity and duplicity of our idolatry. Ultimately, adoption gives us the very thing for which we were made—the triune God who is Father, Son, and Holy Spirit. As Augustine once prayed, "You made us for Yourself, and our heart is restless until it finds its place of rest in You."[9] The only alternatives to finding our satisfaction in the triune God are for us to seek our main sense of identity, significance, and rest either in loose living or in what we do religiously (or missionally)—that is, what we do for the poor and marginalized, for those we consider less fortunate than ourselves.

The glory of our adoption by God is that it gives us the only object of affection (God) that provides rest, satisfies the longing heart, and makes the impoverished unimaginably rich, even in our soul's darkest nights. In other words, adoption gives our restless and fearful hearts the all-satisfying love of the triune God.

In grace *God* has moved outward in mission to bring us into his communion of love forever. You may not have thought about it this way, but God's missional movement into the world *is* his adoptive plan at work. As we enjoy and feed our souls upon the life-giving and perspective-altering truth of our adoption in Christ, we are empowered to do battle daily with our own heart-idolatry. How so, you ask?

The Trinity: Preexistent Authors of Adoption

> But when the fullness of time had come, **God**
> sent forth his **Son**, born of woman, born under
> the law, to redeem those who were under
> the law, so that we might receive adoption as
> sons. And because you are sons, God has sent
> the **Spirit** of his Son into our hearts, crying,
> "Abba! Father!" (Galatians 4:4-6)

By referring to all three Persons of the Trinity,
Galatians 4:4-6 opens a window for us into the core of
ultimate reality. Here we see the Son being sent into the
world and the Spirit being sent into our hearts. Neither
the Son nor the Spirit are created beings; they existed
as eternal members of the Trinity prior to their sending.
What stands behind the mission of God, therefore, and
what moves it forward in the world, is that essential
reality which underlies everything: the communion of
love that is the Holy Trinity.

There was never a moment when the Father, Son,
and Holy Spirit did not exist. There was never an
eternity when they did not exist—eternity past, eternity
present, and eternity future did not, cannot, and will not
exist without them. Not only did all three Persons of
the Trinity preexist the sending of the Son and the Spirit,
they preexist and transcend time itself. They are, after all,
the very foundation of the universe and the intelligent
reason for its existence. Without them, nothing else
ever could or would exist. God's perfectly enjoyed and

unbroken communion of love existed forever before anything was made!

So, as wonderful as the story of our adoption is, it is the Story of the Trinity behind it that gives God's work of adoption its ultimate meaning, beauty, and significance. As John Piper has said, "Adoption is bigger than the universe." How is that true? Because the eternal communion of our triune God is behind, beneath, beside, and above the universe and is the ultimate reason and cause for our adoption. Three quotations from George MacDonald shed light on the significance of this glorious reality:

> The secret of the whole story of humanity is the love between the Father and the Son. That is at the root of it all. Upon the love between the Son and the Father hangs the whole universe.[10]

> The love of God is the creating and redeeming, the forming and satisfying power of the universe . . . It is the safety of the great whole. It is the home-atmosphere of all life.[11]

> The whole of the universe was nothing to Jesus without his Father. The day will come when the whole universe will be nothing to us without the Father, but with the Father an endless glory of delight.[12]

Before the beginning[13] was the eternal communion of the Father, Son, and Holy Spirit, and in the beginning, this triune God—the one true God, eternally existing in three equally divine Persons in communion—created the heavens and the earth. That is the Story behind the story of creation, the story of adoption, and the story of God's gracious mission in the world.

The Trinity: A Necessarily Triune Author

We should not be able to talk about adoption without also talking about this triune God's mission. Adoption is ultimately about relationship, and the relationship that transcends and is the foundation of all others is the relationship(s) that the Persons of the Trinity have eternally enjoyed with each other. Our God has always been and always will be a communion of Persons. Reciprocal love has flowed and will forever flow between the Father, Son, and Holy Spirit. If that reciprocal love ceased for even a moment, God would cease to be God and the gospel would immediately turn into unimaginably bad news for all of creation.

We naturally think of beings as individual, not triune. But Scripture reveals God to be three Persons, not one. Theologians have wrestled with this concept for centuries.[14] Richard of St. Victor, a Scottish theologian of the 12th century, wrote an important philosophical work on the Trinity titled *De Trinitate* (or *On the Trinity*). He combined the teaching found in two passages of Scripture to reach a compelling conclusion. 1) First John 4:8 tells us that God is love. 2) First Corinthians 13 tells us that love never turns in upon itself, but always turns out upon other persons. 3) Therefore, God could not possibly be love if he were only one person.

A god who existed in all eternity past as one person would be a god eternally turned in upon himself. Such a being could not be love because by its nature love turns outward.

Scripture teaches that God is a communion of Persons and has never been a solitary individual. The one triune God has always enjoyed perfect loving communion and joy as three Persons: Father, Son, and Holy Spirit. For all of eternity the Father has loved the Son, the Son has loved the Father, and the Spirit has been the personal bond of that communion. The Father, Son, and Holy Spirit have eternally been and will forever be a communion of Persons.

Think of it this way: God was eternally a closed circle of loving communion (as in an exclusive circle), perfectly satisfied and happy in his triune Being. Even during Jesus' days on earth as the incarnate Son of God, he clearly enjoyed a uniquely close relationship with the Father that everyone else was outside of. In this, we see something of the miraculous and gracious nature of redemption. This fact alone, as theologian Kevin Vanhoozer writes, hints at the striking reality of the gospel which "concerns the triune God's self-communication for the purpose of enlarging the circle of communion. The gospel proclaims a new possibility, namely, that of becoming a 'communicant' in the life of God."[15]

The gospel *begins* with the incomparable good news that when the eternally existing God "predestined us for adoption through Jesus Christ" (Ephesians 1:5), God was an impenetrable closed circle of loving communion. No one could get in and no one wanted to get out. Amazingly, God made the pre-temporal decision to adopt us when all that existed was Father, Son, and Holy Spirit (as if somehow — God forbid! — the Trinity was at a relational disadvantage before that decision was made). Not only did God choose to adopt us before the creation of man but he did so *within* the eternal love ever flowing between the Father and the Son and *within* the all-satisfying communion of the Holy Spirit who is the eternal personal bond of the Father/Son's love (2 Corinthians 13:14). When God made the pre-temporal decision to adopt us, he only knew an infinite relational advantage. Improving upon the communion of love which the triune God eternally enjoyed was an absolute impossibility. It *really* doesn't get better than that. If it could, God would not have been God. But the Trinitarian relationships, which each member enjoyed, were *infinitely beyond the smallest possible degree of improvement.*

This is the astonishing reality with which the gospel's good news begins. As Scottish theologian T.F. Torrance has written, "In his outgoing Love God the Father wills us to coexist appropriately with him as his dear children, and through the presence of his Spirit to share in the Communion of his own eternal Life and Love."[16] What Torrance is saying here can seem too good to be true. But, according to the gospel, it is truer than the air we breathe, truer than gravity, truer than time.

The good news of the gospel is that God's gracious

provision of adoption, irrespective of our grievous demerit, is the activity by which he enlarges the circle of communion that has eternally existed between the three Persons of the Trinity! The joyful news of the gospel is that God the Father brings us to share in the loving communion that he forever enjoys with his eternal and natural Son *through the work* of his eternal and natural Son in our place and in our stead. Through adoption God graciously brings us to participate in the reciprocal love that ever flows between the Father and his Son. Not only is this the very heart of adoption; it is also the very heart of the gospel.

The Trinity: Glad in Community and Glad to Create Community

If God did not need to create man, why did he do it? As we have seen, the creation of man was the free, kind, gracious, intentional overflow of the triune God's joy and love in order to increase the circle of communion and make his glory known. Theologian Douglas Kelly writes, "God sovereignly created the world and placed mankind, his image-bearers, in it, so that they might know him in a community of love, shared life, and obedience."[17] God created us so that we might share in the Trinity's communion to the praise of the glory of his triune grace—for no other reason than that he wanted us to share in it (Ephesians 1:6).

Consider how the creation of mankind is different from that of everything else. Sometime after God's pre-temporal decision to adopt us (Ephesians 1:5), he created the heavens and the earth and, on the sixth day of creation, he made man in his own image (Genesis 1:1, 26-27). The creation week reached its climax when God formed the first man, Adam, from the dust of the ground. God had said, "Let there be" each day of the creation week, but when he created man, he did not say, "Let there be." Instead, God said, "Let us make man in our own image" (Genesis 1:26). When he created man, God's *modus operandi* changed. Something very personal happened when he formed man from the dust of the ground.

Adam and Eve, in contrast to all else God had created, were made in the image of the triune God, in the image of the God who is Father, Son, and Holy Spirit. This means man was not created as a solitary being. Because God is a communion of eternal Persons, and we were made in his triune image, it is clear that we were created to live in communion with other persons—with the Father, Son, and Holy Spirit, and with other human beings. This is central to what it means to be created in the image of God and therefore central to what it means to be on mission with God.[18]

A Theology of Discomfort in a Community of Joy

It is crucial at this point that we understand that our participation in the communion of the Trinity will not move us away from the pain and tragedy of our world. Through adoption we *do* participate daily in the mutual knowing of the Father and the Son. But our participation in God's triune love does not negate our participation in the suffering that the mission of God involves.

In his book, *The Monkey and the Fish: Liquid Leadership for Third Culture Leaders,* Dave Gibbons, a leading missional thinker, provides some insight into the relationship between missional living and what he calls a theology of discomfort.

> The soul of the Great Commission and the Great Commandment leans into difficult people and their complexities. It's to be the essence of who we are as Christians. In fact, unity of mind and generosity of spirit in the midst of diversity is the distinguishing mark of true Christian community.
>
> It's a bold, radical endeavor: to love our neighbor. But it's the endeavor God has called us to. It's where the gospel becomes real. It really speaks to the power of Jesus if we can work through our discomfort and overcome the barriers we too easily let divide us.
>
> This concept, this theology of discomfort, can be seen throughout the Scriptures, both in the Old and New Testaments. So much so it makes me realize how often we can know what is right but practice what is merely expedient.
>
> Throughout the Old Testament we hear that we are to radically love outsiders, widows, and orphans, to act as a voice for the voiceless, and to be a father to the fatherless. In Corinthians we see God saying he focuses on the weak of this world to speak to the mighty. In John 14, Jesus explains to the disciples that obeying him and loving the "least of these" in society give us deep understanding about him and his ways.[19]

A theology of discomfort and its relationship to missional living is ultimately grounded in the example of the Father sending his Son into the world (Galatians 4:4-6). T.F. Torrance writes:

> Through the *coming* of Jesus Christ into the world as the only begotten Son loved by the Father, the Love which flows eternally between the Father and the Son in the Holy Trinity has moved outward to bear upon us in history and *is made known to us above all in the sacrificial love of Jesus in laying down his life for us* (emphasis mine).[20]

When the eternal Son of God became man, he ushered his infinite, flawless communion with the Father into the depths of our sin, pain, and suffering (see Mark 14:36), not impersonally but in a profoundly personal manner. Jesus' communion with the Father and the Spirit did not detach or distance him from the brokenness of our world. To the contrary, it thrust him into the darkest depths of our fallen world in order that he might heal and deliver us through his death, burial, and resurrection.

At what point did the Father declare, "This is my beloved Son, with whom I am well pleased"? It was just before the Spirit led Jesus "into the wilderness to be tempted by the devil" (Matthew 3:17-4:1). The Trinitarian enjoyment of communion did not lead Jesus away from suffering but into it. According to T.F. Torrance,

> [W]e learn from [Jesus'] incarnate self-revelation

that God does not will to exist for himself alone and does not wish to be without us, but has in his eternal purpose of love freely created a universe, within which he has placed human beings made after his own image and likeness in order that he may share his love with them and enable them to enjoy his divine fellowship.[21]

No suffering for Jesus, no enjoyment of divine fellowship for us. Jesus' redemptive achievement in our place and on our behalf, then, is why "obeying him and loving the 'least of these' in society give us deep understanding about him and his ways."[22]

In his wonderfully mysterious wisdom God leads us into suffering as we participate in the Trinity's communion of love, but he also makes our experience of that suffering the occasion for our deepest enjoyment of his love. How is this possible? *Because to share in the sufferings of Jesus* (Philippians 3:10) *is to share in the goal of his suffering*: the enjoyment of his divine fellowship. As we participate in the mission of God, our suffering never happens in isolation from Jesus. Believers who are on mission always suffer in union with Jesus.

Mission in the Context of Divine Community

Scripture's teaching on the Trinity calls us to find our rest in the Trinity's communion of love, not in the predictable, fleeting stories of our own making. When all we can see are our own self-written, self-directed stories, shot through with idolatry and brokenness, we will reject the rigors of true missional engagement. But as we daily rediscover that in Christ we are the Father's beloved children, with whom he is well pleased, we can faithfully obey the Father and love the least of these.

> To know this God, who both condescends to share all that we are and makes us share in all that he is in Jesus Christ, is to be lifted up in his Spirit to share in God's own self-knowing and self-loving until we are enabled to apprehend him in some real measure in himself beyond anything that we are capable of in ourselves. It is to be lifted out of ourselves, as it were, into God, until we know him and love him and enjoy him in his eternal Reality as Father, Son, and Holy Spirit in such a way that the Trinity enters into the fundamental fabric of our thinking of him and constitutes the basic grammar of our worship and knowledge of the One God...[23]

Let us take Torrance's point one logical step further. As the wonders of our relationship with and in the Trinity, through Christ, come to form the "basic grammar" of our worship and knowledge of God, they will also come to form the basic grammar of our participation in his mission.

Three
ADOPTION AND THE INCARNATION

Dan Cruver

My work in the world of orphan care and adoption provides me regular opportunities to travel internationally. When I visit orphans, I bring their stories back home and share them as widely as possible. My hope and prayer is that Christians who hear these stories will come to understand the needs, begin to put a face on James 1:27, and become actively engaged in "visiting orphans in their distress."

In January of 2008 I traveled to Ethiopia, one of the poorest and most underdeveloped countries in the world. Nearly 18 percent of Ethiopian children—an estimated 6,230,000 of them—have lost one or both parents to poverty and disease. These children are ten times more likely to suffer from infectious disease, HIV/AIDS, and human trafficking.

The statistics are alarming, but the reality is worse.

On top of everything else, the sense of spiritual oppression in that country can at times be overwhelming. It reminds me of being surrounded by a house full of sick family members—you're well enough yourself, but you sense your vulnerability and recognize that your own health could break at any moment.

In the months prior to this trip, God had given me the privilege of getting to know Anthony Mathenia and his family. Anthony is an American who trains Ethiopian church planters, has two adopted Ethiopian children, and is very knowledgeable about that country's orphan crisis. More than that, it was obvious to me that he loves the people of Ethiopia deeply, and he lives out that love. I soon found myself hoping that I would learn to give myself to others half as well as he.

Anthony joined us on that January trip. I wanted to learn as much from him as I could, so I was delighted when he wanted to stay a little longer to introduce us to the people and land he had come to love. After serving as our guide for three additional days, Anthony flew home to rejoin his family after a separation of a week and a half.

The next day my cell phone rang. Anthony was calling from Tennessee. His voice was broken and at first all he did was repeat my name several times. Finally, he was able to speak. As if in a bad dream, I heard him tell me that shortly after his plane had left the ground in Africa, his wife had been killed in a car accident. He'd only received the horrific news after landing in Memphis.

The nightmare of that phone call didn't end when I said goodbye to my grief-stricken friend. It got worse.

*If this could happen to Anthony—as faithful as he has been to the gospel and to the people of Ethiopia—it could happen to my family and me. As a matter of fact, it **should** happen to me.*

This last thought somehow took hold of me. Over the next several days, the sinister whisper in my head steadily evolved into a dark night in my soul.

Right after the phone call, we needed to leave our hotel to drive to an orphanage in Shashemene, but as we traveled I could not stop thinking of Anthony or silence the evil whisper in my mind. Two questions haunted me: *Why did this happen to Anthony? Will it happen to me and my family?*

I entered the orphanage with these questions pounding in my head, only to be met by ninety children who had either been abandoned by their parents or lost one or both parents. These children knew what it meant to be alone, plagued by memories of death or rejection. They were the reason I had traveled all this way. But all I could experience in that moment was my own struggle. I hardly even noticed theirs.

As I walked through that orphanage, tangled up in my fear, I actually found myself becoming afraid of God. Words like those of Job 23:13-17 began to weigh upon me:

> But [God] is unchangeable, and who can turn him
> back?
> What he desires, that he does.
> For he will complete what he appoints for me,
> and many such things are in his mind.

> Therefore I am terrified at his presence;
> when I consider, I am in dread of him.
> God has made my heart faint;
> the Almighty has terrified me;
> yet I am not silenced because of the darkness,
> nor because thick darkness covers my face.

During the next few days, a dark cloud of nearly paralyzing fear gathered around me, only getting worse as I prepared for my trip back home. As I took my seat on board the plane in Addis Ababa for the first leg of that trip, my adrenalin began to surge. The plane appeared to shrink, and I became convinced we were going to crash. For the first time in my life, I was terrified of flying.

During the flight I tried everything I could think of to get my mind off the fact that I was 33,000 feet over the Sahara, traveling at hundreds of miles an hour, and separated from death by a few inches and a thin skin of aluminum. Desperate for distraction, I pulled a copy of *People* magazine from the seat pocket in front of me. As I opened it my eyes fell on the headline, "Heath Ledger Found Dead."

It took six flights for me to get home—six flights and the only six anxiety attacks I have ever had. Each flight was haunted by a sense of peril and doom unlike anything I had ever known.

You are going to die on this plane. It will certainly crash, and when it does, you will die. You will die...and you will go to hell.

Every effort to free myself from these dark thoughts only pulled me in further.

Dan, the gospel is not for you. You are as much beyond its reach as those who have died without Christ. Yes, the gospel is good news . . . but it is not for you.

Suddenly, Jesus' call in Matthew 16:24 to deny myself "and take up [my] cross and follow" him terrified me — I knew I did not have in myself the ability to abandon all and follow Jesus to death. When Jesus commanded the rich young ruler to follow him, Matthew writes that "he went away sorrowful, for he had great possessions" (Matthew 19:22). For me, in that plane, I was tempted to go away sorrowful because I treasured my life and feared physical death.

Joy in the gospel had been replaced with dread. Missional engagement had been vanquished by self-preoccupation. I went to Ethiopia with the determination to serve orphans. I left there able to think only of myself. My paralysis was both personal and missional.

Is There Another God Behind Jesus?

T. F. Torrance served as a stretcher-bearer on the front lines during World War II. On one occasion he came upon a mortally wounded soldier who was conscious but near death. As the blood poured out of the terrified young soldier, he looked up into Torrance's eyes and asked, "Padre, is God really like Jesus?"[24] According to Torrance, that young soldier was essentially asking: "Is there another god behind the back of Jesus?" In other words, is God one thing in himself and another thing in Jesus Christ?[25] That was the same basic question that I was wrestling with on my way home from Ethiopia.

If the God of the Bible is three gods and not one God, then we are left with the doubts that lay beneath that young soldier's question. And when we can ask that question, we will also ask, "Padre, is Jesus really like the God who is said to be love? Can he really be trusted? Can I risk following him to death?" We may not ask such questions when our lives are comfortable, but when confronted with our own mortality or a "dark night of the soul," our questions can become haunting and inescapable.

My imaginary fears, as well as the very real ones suffered by that young soldier, were due to the same misperception. We were not relating to God as Trinity. If the Father, Son, and Holy Spirit are three gods, then the soldier's question and my fears would be legitimate. If there are three gods and not one, we could not be assured that what we get with one we also get with the other two. Even if we knew what one of them thought of us, we would always be looking over our shoulder for the other two. Three distinct gods is not good news for sinners.

But there is good news, and it begins with the fact that God has always, does now, and will always relate to us as *Trinity*, one true God eternally existing as three co-equal Persons in divine communion. In the midst of my dark night of the soul, God began to bring me relief by graciously reminding me through Scripture's teaching on adoption that God is Triune and always relates to me as such.

The Centrality of the Incarnation

At the heart of God's Triune dealings with humanity is the incarnation of the second Person of the Trinity. To neglect this fact—especially when confronted with a "frowning providence"—is to set ourselves up for personal and missional paralysis. Our eyes become locked in on ourselves and it becomes nearly impossible to move outward in genuine mission. But even through the greatest trials, the profound reality of the incarnation can overcome our paralysis, empower us to persevere, and move us forward in love to others.

Jesus tells us that "no one knows the Son except the Father, and no one knows the Father except the Son and anyone to whom the Son chooses to reveal him" (Matthew 11:27). The relationship between the Father and the Son is so exclusive that they alone hold the relational key to one another.

Consider also Jesus' words, "I and the Father are one" (John 10:30), and later, "I am the way, and the truth, and the life. No one comes to the Father except through me" (John 14:6). Jesus is the center of man's knowledge and interaction with the Father. Christ is not only the Way and the Truth of communion with the Father, he is the Life—the source of knowing for us. Practically, this means that we must never think of the Father or seek to relate to him apart from Jesus. We do not have that right; no one does. Access to the Father is only through the Son.

Only when we acknowledge the utter exclusivity of Trinitarian relationships can we truly appreciate what God has given us in adoption. What was the Son's missional objective when God sent him to secure our adoption (Galatians 4:4-5)? Theologian Douglas Kelly provides the amazing answer: "The Son has come down to earth to do all that was necessary to lift us up to a true knowledge of the Father, so that we share in the Son's knowledge of the Father."[26] The Son's missional objective in adoption was to bring prodigals to participate in *his* knowing of the Father—not some generic knowing of God but into the Son's knowing of God as Father.

Clearly, the incarnate Son is the axis upon which the Trinity's dealings with us revolve. Jesus, as God of gods and a Man among men, is the place where man and God meet. The stories of the Trinity and the incarnation belong together. Separate them, and the gospel is no longer good news for fallen man. Separate them, and suddenly another god appears behind the back of Jesus, one who cannot be trusted or known. Separate them, and we have a recipe for personal and missional paralysis.

Communion as the Light for Dark Nights

What tangible help do these truths provide us when we are experiencing a dark night of the soul? Don't forget, as we saw in Chapter One, that the story of the Trinity is behind the story of the Prodigal Son(s). The existence of the triune God is what makes that parable good news for us: Prodigals can experience the extravagant love of God as Father, through the incarnate Son, as the Holy Spirit applies his work to our dead hearts.

In his genealogy of Jesus, Luke identifies Adam as "the son of God" (Luke 3:38).[27] Simply stated, God created Adam to be his son: not a divine son in any way, for there is only one divine Son, but a son who bore the image of God as a creature. Sinclair Ferguson explains this:

> To be a son, in the language of Genesis, was to be made in the image and likeness of one's father. . . To be a son, and to be the image and likeness of your father, are synonymous ideas. To put it another way, if we wish to understand what man was intended to be, we need to think of him as a son of God.[28]

God's original intention for humanity—his original intention for us—was that we were to be his beloved sons, his cherished children. As God's image-bearers, we were created in the beginning to participate in the love that ever flows between God the Father and God the Son, and to participate in that love on the earth as our happy home. But in rebellion, God's son (small *s*) left the Father's house in his heart even before he was expelled from the Father's presence physically. In Adam, we all exchanged the love of the Father for the things of the Father (Romans 1:23, 25)—just as the prodigal sons did in Luke 15—and by virtue of that tragic exchange, we suddenly found ourselves in the far country of our own self-inflicted estrangement, alienation, and antagonism against God. When we were supposed to live on earth in God's presence as children of his love, we became "sons of disobedience" and "children of wrath" (Ephesians 2:2-3) and lived "east of Eden" just as Cain did (Genesis 4:16).

Through Adam's sin, conflict with God replaced communion, and that conflict became deeply embedded into our inmost being. As a result, we are by nature enslaved to the objects of our misplaced love (Galatians 4:3, 8). As the 19th Century German philosopher Friedrich Nietzsche has written, "There are more idols in the world than there are realities."[29] Because of our idolatry, none of us is truly able to abandon all and take up our cross to follow Jesus. Our estrangement from the Father affects us the same way it affected the rich young ruler (Matthew 19:16-22): We turn away. Like the prodigals in Luke 15, we manifest our estrangement "either by breaking [God's] rules or by keeping all of them diligently."[30] Behind the externals of both prodigal rule-breaking and prodigal rule-keeping (or any combination of the two) is estrangement from the Father. In the end, both rule-keepers and rule-breakers turn away from God's radical and justly binding demands upon our lives.

At this point, it is critically important that we remember that the Son, who was sent forth to redeem us so that we might receive adoption as sons, is none other than the One who not only eternally enjoyed communion with the Father but also fulfilled all the Father's will. The Son who was sent is a member of the Trinity that has been, is, and forever will be a communion of Persons. Therefore, when that Son became incarnate, *communion with God became incarnate, and with his incarnation perfect obedience permanently entered the human race in him*. In the incarnate Son, communion with the Father and perfect obedience to his holy will finally burst into the far country of our alienation from the Father. Through the incarnation, Jesus (fully God and fully man in his one Person) became not merely the means but the place—the locale—where communion with and obedience to God happens in all its unimaginable fullness. It is only in the Person of Christ that God and man meet in loving communion. The understated good news of the gospel is that *the humanity of Jesus has become our communion with and obedience to his Father*. Only in Jesus can true radical obedience and unending communion be found.

The Son of God came into the far country of our estrangement, not as an outsider or a detached observer, but as a true man among men, like us in every respect yet without sin (Hebrews 2:17; 4:15). James Torrance (younger brother to T.F. and a theologian himself) explains it this way:

> Christ does not heal us by standing over against us, diagnosing our sickness, prescribing medicine for us to take, and then going away, to leave us to get better by obeying his instructions—as an ordinary doctor

might. No, he becomes the patient! He assumes that very humanity which is in need of redemption, and by being anointed by the Spirit in our humanity, by a life of perfect obedience for us, by dying and rising again, our humanity is healed in him.[31]

By being "born of a woman" (Galatians 4:4), the Son of God journeyed into the far country that he might heal us of our estrangement and conflict with God *from within his own Person*. As soon as Jesus was conceived by the Spirit in the virgin womb of Mary, the healing and sanctifying of our humanity began. When Jesus said, "I am the resurrection and the life" (John 11:25), he was not merely referring to what he was about to do with Lazarus in the tomb, nor to what he would ultimately do in the last day, but to the entirety of his incarnate life. Jesus was the Resurrection and the Life from the moment he was conceived in the virgin womb all the way to his resurrection from the dead and forever beyond. It was from that very moment that he began to heal and sanctify our humanity—to progressively bring his resurrection life to bear upon all our inability, estrangement and disobedience—from the inside out.

By being "born under the law" (Galatians 4:4), Jesus lived out a life of perfect communion with the Father in our place, as our substitute. What we did not do in the Garden of Eden, and what we do not do now, he did for us in the far country outside the Garden in his incarnate Person that he might bring us home to the Father *in himself*. Jesus' humanity has become the place of our communion with God. By virtue of his union with us and our subsequent union with him by the Spirit, we are amazingly and wonderfully brought to participate in his knowing of the Father. In other words, Jesus is where our communion with the Father happens, and Jesus is the *only* place where it happens.

Resurrection as the Rescue from Dark Nights

We must return to this question again: What practical help does the Incarnation provide us when we are experiencing the dark night of the soul? How did God use the reality of the Incarnation to bring me out of the dark cloud of paralyzing fear that had engulfed me? How is the gospel freeing me from my fear to abandon all and follow Jesus even unto death? One fact lies behind each answer: When Jesus entered the far country of my estrangement from God, he did not journey just inside its borders. He journeyed into its very heart and brought with him resurrection power.

A dark night of the soul needs resurrection power because it feels like a kind of death. John Calvin described "the death of the soul" this way: "It is to be without God—to be abandoned by God, and left to itself: for if God is its life, it loses its life when it loses the presence of God."[32]

When that fear descended upon me in Ethiopia, I felt as if I had lost the very presence of God—the one thing that I needed most, the one thing without which I could not live. But when Jesus became man and entered into the far country, which is our estrangement from God, he was truly forsaken by God in my place without ceasing to be God for even a fraction of a moment. As the God-man, not only did Jesus become my obedience, my faith, my prayer, my love to the Father, my feelings of joy in the Father, but he also became my forsakenness—*without ceasing to be God*. He took up *my* cross, abandoned all, and "became obedient to the point of death, even death on a cross (Philippians 2:8), and he did this for me, in my place. Not only did Jesus do for me what I cannot do for myself, he also did for his twelve disciples what they could not do for themselves, namely, offer the Father radical obedience. All of Jesus' original disciples eventually turned away from him as he approached his crucifixion (Mark 14:50). The good news of the gospel is that Jesus took up our cross and obediently and wholeheartedly followed his Father to death for us and in our place without ever ceasing to be God.

This matter of not ceasing to be God is absolutely critical if the news upon which we hang all our hopes is indeed "good." Even when he was forsaken by God, Jesus never ceased to be God. Why is this important to the gospel? T.F. Torrance points us to the answer:

> [Jesus] met the full opposition of our enmity to God, and the full opposition of God to our enmity and endured it with joy, refusing to let go of God for our sakes, and refusing to let go of us for God's sake. In laying hold of us as sinners, he judged our sin in

himself and reconciled us to God, and in laying hold of God he received his judgment of us upon himself and offered our humanity in himself to the Father.[33]

Only a triune God could both refuse "to let go of God for our sakes" and refuse "to let go of us for God's sake." Only a triune God could lay hold of God and offer our humanity in himself to the Father. Take God out of the cross even for a nanosecond and redemption unto adoption does not happen.

Jesus, Our All

My fear of flying continues, though not nearly so intense as on my return from Ethiopia. Even as I write this I can feel the darkening cloud of anxiety attempt to descend upon my heart as I think about the fact that I have to fly to Chicago in two days to speak on orphan care at a church. I am beginning to see flying as an opportunity to cast myself afresh upon the Son of God, who by the Spirit joined himself to my humanity, became my obedience, my faith, my prayer, my love to the Father, my abandonment to a life of sacrificial living, and my God-forsakenness…without ever ceasing to be God.

As God graciously continues to open the eyes of my heart to all that Jesus was and is for me in his own Person and in his life and death, the cloud of fear that once engulfed me lifts. Throughout the whole course of his life, Jesus was everything for me, both from the side of God and from the side of man in his very own Person.

My security in the midst of doubt and fear does not lie in my ability to find my way out of dark thoughts, or my human efforts to abandon all for the sake of the kingdom and missional living. It lies in who Jesus was for me in his own Person through the whole course of his incarnate life.

"Abandon all, take up your cross and follow me." If in responding to this command our stress is primarily upon our own responsibility, we will first look within, at the quality and sincerity of our own faith and repentance, rather than without, at the vicarious life and death of Christ. "Gospel proclamation" that leads Christians to think mainly about *what they must do*, rather than mainly about *what Jesus has done* as our substitute inclines the hearers to stray from gospel-centered missional living.

The good news of the gospel is that Jesus has done it all—*for* us and *in* our place. Only as we believe and live in the reality of what he has done are we progressively freed to live truly missional and radically obedient lives in a broken world.

As we grow in understanding the reality of who Jesus is for us, we are progressively freed from our personal and missional paralysis and empowered to turn outward for the gospel-good of others. The good news of who Jesus was and is for us as the God-man turns dread into joy and frees us from self-preoccupation to move outward in mission.

Four
ADOPTION AND OUR UNION WITH CHRIST

Dan Cruver

I have learned that if I am not careful, I can find my primary identity in who I am (my roles) and in what I do (my responsibilities). Nearly everything in the prevailing culture—including a great deal in Christian culture—presses me in this direction and affirms it as *the* way to think about my life.

Certainly these things are important, for they are essential to what it means for me to be human. The problem is one of emphasis and hierarchy. As a Christian, my *primary* sense of identity, my *controlling* sense of identity, is to be found in who Jesus is and who I am in relationship to him. In fact, only when my primary identity is in Christ can my true humanity be preserved, for only then are my roles and responsibilities—my secondary identities—rightly positioned under him.

Apart from who Jesus is and who I am in

relationship with him, my humanity becomes either a source of confidence (producing self-reliance and pride) or a source of discouragement (weakening hope and faith, and producing ingratitude toward God). This is why I try to begin each day by asking myself: "Who is Jesus?" and "Who am I in relationship with him?" This helps me keep Christ at the center of each day rather than myself—not my problems, not my struggles, not even my successes.

If Jesus is the center and meaning of the universe (Colossians 1:15-20), and if Jesus was *for me* the person I have not been or ever could be on my own, then beginning each day by asking those two questions seems like a very good thing to do.

Our Bond to Christ and in Christ

Among Christians, adoption (the vertical and *then* the horizontal) is beginning to get more of the attention it deserves. Lagging well behind it in attention, however, is the fascinating and closely related subject of our union with Christ. Ephesians 1:5-6 gives us a glimpse of how tightly these two concepts are joined. "[God the Father] predestined us for adoption as sons through Jesus Christ, according to the purpose of his will, to the praise of his glorious grace, with which he has blessed us in the Beloved."

Consider for a moment that the Greek word for the term *adoption* that Paul uses is a compound of the words for "son" and "to place." Together they render the word as meaning "placement as a son."[34] Now, notice that Paul says we have been predestined "for adoption as sons through Jesus Christ" and then he informs us that this blessing of adoption was given to us "in the Beloved." By putting these concepts back to back, Paul is revealing that adoption was not given to us *apart from* or *in isolation from* Jesus. Nor was it given to us *in addition to* Jesus. Rather, adoption is nothing less than **the placement of sons in the Son**. These two concepts—adoption unto the Father, and being in Christ—are so necessarily joined to one another as to be inseparable.

Personally, I suspect that Paul intentionally used "adoption" as a shorthand or code word for our union with Christ. Adoption and union are that closely joined.

- If we can be *adopted* without being *in Christ*, there is no need for Jesus.
- If we can be *in Christ* without being *adopted* by the Father, there is no Trinity.
- If adoption and union with Christ are not essentially the same thing, there is no gospel.

One way to think about what it means to be "in Christ" is to consider what theologians call the "double binding" between Christ and his redeemed. The first binding refers to how Jesus, in his incarnation, joined himself to us by taking on flesh, thus becoming man with us. This union of the Son of God with our humanity was essential to our subsequent union with Christ—the second binding. The first binding (the joining of the Son with us) made possible the second binding (the joining of us with the Son).

The Son of God became the Son of Man that we might become adopted sons of God in union with him.

The Ministry of the Son

The great Dutch theologian Herman Ridderbos writes that our union with Christ is not a reality that "becomes reality only in certain sublime moments, but rather [is] an abiding reality determinative for the whole of the Christian life."[35] Do not miss that word, *determinative*. We must not think of our union with Christ as only involving "spiritually oriented" activities. Rather, it is *the* reality that should shape and determine the entirety of our Christian lives.

For Christians, the reality of our union with Christ means that we never do anything independently of him. The Christian life is not Jesus doing one thing in heaven at the right hand of the Father while we do our thing here on earth. Our union with Christ is indissoluble, unceasing, and determinative at all times and in all places. There is never the smallest fraction of a fraction of a second when we are not living and moving and having our being in union with Jesus. For the believer, union with Christ is everything.

As the letter to the Hebrews teaches, Jesus is the resurrected and ascended Minister (8:1-2) who not only purifies and cleanses our Christian ministry but also leads it. Since Jesus leads our service in the kingdom of God (Hebrews 12:28) and has gathered us up into union with himself, what Jesus does *now*, we do.

The Ministry of the Sons

This means that, at its source, missional engagement is not really what we do at all. It is what Jesus does. God is always the initiator. Jesus engages us in mission; we do not engage him.

Our missional engagement as Christians is not an imitation *of* Christ and his mission. It is a participation *in* Christ and his mission. This is not wordplay. It is a polar shift of perspective from the false to the true, and from the self-centered to the Christ-centered. The difference between the two perspectives is almost impossible to overstate. After all, "There is only one ministry, that of Jesus Christ, to which through union with Christ we are joined."[36]

Put another way, our efforts do not consist in a striving to imitate Christ. They *result* in the imitation of Christ as we participate with him in his mission in the world. Seeing this can make a huge difference in how we live. If we understand our union with Christ well, it will change our perspective such that we will live missionally. The writers of the New Testament assume this kind of living. When, over and over, you see Paul using the phrases "in Christ"[37] and "in him,"[38] recognize that he means for Christians to think about every aspect of their lives in terms of union with Christ. Our activity is a participation in what he is already doing (Galatians 2:20).

Missional engagement is not primarily about engaging culture, as important as it is to do so, but about seeing people brought into communion with God. Therefore, our missional engagement in the world must be driven and marked by our enjoyment of communion with our triune God and with each other as a community of faith. Nothing surpasses the power of our union with and adoption in Christ to inform, shape, and empower this gospel-centered practice of missional living.

The reality of this astounding truth should both humble and energize us. It should humble us by reminding us that missional engagement is not *our* ministry. If it were, we would all be in big trouble, because we really do not serve others all that well. Sometimes we even seem to fail miserably. But as we labor in Christ's ministry, in participation with him, we are united with God's appointed Leader for every God-ordained ministry (Hebrews 5:5). Because of that unity, Jesus gathers up all that we do missionally into himself, purifying, cleansing, and transforming it so that all we do for him really matters and has eternal significance. That's humbling, in a very good way.

We should be energized for the same reasons we are humbled. Because missional engagement is primarily the ministry of Jesus, through union with him we participate in what he does. *This guarantees effectiveness!* What we do missionally matters—really matters—eternally. Even when we are "off our game," Jesus takes our five loaves and two fish (Matthew 14:19) and multiplies them exponentially. When we engage missionally, it's never just us, or even primarily us: it's Jesus!

If anything will mobilize us as Christians for long-term missional engagement, it will be a deeper understanding and appreciation of our union with Christ.

Identity

This returns us to those two questions I try to ask myself every morning: "Who is Jesus?" and "Who am I in relationship with him?" Here are the *Cliff's Notes* versions of my answers.

Who is Jesus? Jesus is the one place—the only place—where God and man meet, perfectly and eternally. Not only is Jesus one in being with the Father, he is also forevermore one with humanity: when the Son became man, made among men in the likeness of sinful flesh (Romans 8:3), he "came forth as true man and took the person and name of Adam in order to take Adam's place in obeying the Father."[39] In the Person of Jesus, then, reconciliation between God and man was worked out for us during the whole course of his life, climaxing at his cross, his resurrection, and his ascension. Everything wrong with our humanity has been made right and restored in Jesus. In him, we find a true resurrected man enjoying perfect, unbroken communion with the Father, exercising dominion over the world as God originally intended, and existing totally free from every effect of the fall. Because of the gospel we are united with this Jesus—the one who blessed children, touched lepers, loved the marginalized, cared for the "least of these," succeeded in all the ways the we fail, and said to his disciples and to all who would follow after them, "I will not leave you as orphans; I will come to you" (John 14:18).

Who are we in relationship with Jesus? Jesus is the Savior who in saving us has become our brother. By being in him, we have become adopted into the family of the Father. By virtue of who Jesus is in his incarnate Person, my reality is that I actually (not mythically!), participate in *his* resurrected life, *his* uncompromising, unconditional abandonment to perfect obedience, *his* present communion with the Father, and *his* ongoing mission in the world.

If you have been adopted in the Beloved, that is your reality as well, and it has everything to do with how you live each day. Your adoption by God in Christ is not just for security today and forever; it is also for your empowerment in God's mission, today and forever.

Our missional work to serve the lost, the broken, the marginalized, the orphan, the widow, and everyone else who needs God's grace and mercy has been carried in Christ to the very throne of God. All that we do missionally is done in union with our brother, the man Christ Jesus. I cannot think of anything better to humble, mobilize, and energize Christians than this stunning reality. This is our adoption. Glory in it. Be daily humbled and energized by it.

Five

THE GOOD NEWS OF ADOPTION

Richard D. Phillips

Contemporary evangelicals are hampered by a defect or imbalance in practical doctrine, or how we think about Christianity. Many of us seem stagnant because we have no sense of purpose. We understand that we are sinners saved from God by God. By this we mean that God has a just wrath against sin, and we know that God's grace in the incarnation and death and resurrection of Jesus Christ saves us *from* that wrath. We know what we have been saved *from*, but we do not know how to live in the present age. This is because we do not fully understand what it means that we have been saved *to* God. That is, we do not really understand our adoption in Christ.

The Bible robustly describes the relationship we can have with God, and this relationship seems rather important to us. These days, many beleivers think of having a sentimental relationship with God or a spiritual relationship with God in a way that we experience but cannot really define or think about carefully. But in Ephesians, we see a clear definition of what God has declared about our personal relationship with him. If we will fully embrace what God's Word teaches about what we have been saved *to*—the structure, content, privileges, and obligations of our personal relationship with God—our experience of the gospel will be revolutionized.

We have been saved *to* God *through* adoption. And what a great thing the truth of adoption is! When we see the biblical doctrine of adoption clearly, we see that it must affect how we think about our relationship to God. Our heavenly Father displays his love, grace, and glory uniquely through his adoption of sons and daughters.

The Eternal Foundations of Adoption

Paul begins his letter to the Ephesians with a hymn of praise to the God and Father of our Lord Jesus Christ. He praises God for all the blessings we have in Jesus Christ, his Son. He begins by unfolding the doctrine of election, or predestination, and thereby focuses on the eternal foundations of our salvation blessings.

Blessed be the God and Father of our Lord Jesus Christ, who has blessed us in Christ with every spiritual blessing in the heavenly places, even as he chose us in him before the foundation of the world, that we should be holy and blameless before him. In love he predestined us for adoption as sons through Jesus Christ, according to the purpose of his will, to the praise of his glorious grace, with which he has blessed us in the Beloved. (Ephesians 1:3-6)

I ministered for many years at Tenth Presbyterian Church in downtown Philadelphia, Pennsylvania. For the last two years we were there, the tallest skyscraper in Philadelphia was being built. I passed the construction site almost daily, and it was not impressive. I figured that watching people build a skyscraper would be fascinating, but most days I looked at the site, I could see nothing but a hole in the ground. Occasionally I would ask a worker about what was going on, and he would say, "We're laying the foundation." For two years, they worked underground laying the foundation.

Paul has a similar way of thinking in Ephesians 1. He wants us to know the eternal foundations of our relationship with God—the purpose, the will, the decree, the counsel, the predestination, the election of God. God laid that foundation in eternity, just like you had better lay a strong and deep foundation to put up a 58-story skyscraper. God is building a salvation kingdom that stretches upwards infinitely, so he digs eternally deep foundations.

What are those eternal foundations? God has counseled and predestined various blessings at the base of his relationship with us. First comes election: the glorious truth that God chose you in Christ. He chose you for holiness, for forgiveness, and to know the mystery of his will. If you are in Christ, you have been chosen by God and predestined in Christ. If you believe in Jesus Christ as Lord and Savior, God has willed your adoption.

The Privileges of Adoption

Paul uses the term *adoption* as drawn from the legal context of the Roman Empire. In Paul's day, adoption was an important feature of the Roman world, and it carried no stigma; on the contrary, it was special to have been adopted. It meant that someone important had set his love upon you and adopted you to be his son, his heir.

We must therefore distinguish adoption from regeneration. They are related because we need the status as sons and daughters of God and also we need our nature changed in order to live as such, but our relationship to God as adopted children with all the rights of heirs is not based upon our sanctification. Instead, adoption is simply a legal change of status: if you believe in the Lord Jesus Christ, God has bestowed upon you the status of son of the most high God. This status does not depend on whether you did your devotions or how you feel about yourself: it is a legal declaration, a change in status.

Similarly, Roman adoption indicated a radical break with the past. All previous debts were eradicated, and all previous allegiances were erased. An adopted person became completely new, just as we experience in Christ. We are still capable of acting according to the old identity in sin, but this is disgraceful and ungrateful. Adoption means full membership in God's family: God has one natural begotten Son, the Lord Jesus, and all of his children through adoption also have full membership in his affections and full participation in his family. We are, as it says in Ephesians 5:1, God's "beloved children"! Because God has a great love within himself, because he purposed in eternity to adopt sons and daughters who know him as their heavenly Father, we can truly know that we are dearly beloved, not second-class members of the family.

Contemporary adoption certificates can teach us here. A legal adoption certificate from the state of Pennsylvania says, "Said adoptee shall have all the rights of a child and shall be heir of the adoptive parents and shall be subject to all the duties of a child." So too, as God's children through adoption, we have all the rights and duties of God's children, and we are heirs of the Father.

The Privilege of Prayer: Personal Relationship with Our Heavenly Father

Adopted children of God have the right to a relationship in which we can actually access God as Father. The God of the universe invites you to call him "Daddy." Jesus invited us to pray to God as our Father because we have access to God as such. Paul says in Ephesians 2 that through Jesus and by his blood on the cross we have access in the Holy Spirit to God *the Father*. If the Son saves you to the Father, you now have a personal relationship with his Father. This relationship is the basis for prayer. If you are a believer in Jesus Christ and you know you are adopted in the Beloved, then you come to God the way a child goes to a loving father, saying "Father, may I talk to you?" God the Father longs for you to talk to him, and you have access to him in Jesus Christ. What makes your prayer effective is God's love for you and his bond to you in the gospel.

In Luke 11, Jesus teaches the Lord's Prayer and then two parables about prayer. In the second parable Jesus argues that even bad fathers generally grant the requests of their children, so how much more will our heavenly Father grant things to you? God has taken upon himself the obligation to be our Father; his honor, his dignity, and his glory drive him to hear our prayers. So in prayer, we must believe that we are children of God, with all the rights of children through the great grace of adoption. Adoption opens your access to your Father.

The Privilege of Provision: Personal Care from Our Heavenly Father

Not only does our adoption secure our access to God as our Father in prayer, but through adoption, God takes upon himself the obligation of our care and provision in this life. This does not mean we will have no trials: God is no great Santa Claus who only desires temporal prosperity for us in a materialistic paradise. It means something much better than that: God the Father will be involved with your life. David says with a straight face that he has never seen the people of God really destitute, because God cares for them (Psalm 37:25). God takes care of our greatest needs: righteousness, peace, joy, faith, hope, love. We are children with a Father we can look to and pray to, confidently knowing that he has taken the obligation to care for us, even in death. All through our lives and even beyond, we can be sure of God's loving care and provision. The answer to all our struggles and anxieties is God's Fatherhood. We must take rest in the assurance that God will minister to us out of his love for us.

The Privilege of Discipline: Personal Holiness from Our Heavenly Father

We have access to God who cares for us and provides for us, but as adopted sons and daughters of God we also enjoy the privilege of discipline. This may not seem like a privilege, but God thinks of it that way because it reveals another aspect of how he is involved in the lives of his children. According to Hebrews 12, God disciplines us as sons for a harvest of righteousness.

More than anything else, God wants holiness from us, but we generally prefer happiness. We want the good, but God wants glory in our lives. The good news is that we have a Father who loves us enough to bring us better things than we want for ourselves. C. S. Lewis put it this way: "We are half-hearted creatures, fooling about with drink and sex and ambition when infinite joy is offered us, like an ignorant child who wants to go on making mud pies in a slum because he cannot imagine what is meant by the offer of a holiday at the sea. We are far too easily pleased."[40]

Isn't that the story of America? We settle for video entertainment, for drugs of all kinds, when God would have us know him, showing us his glory and calling us to himself. Indeed, we are seeing revival in some evangelicals today: God is raising up young people who truly want to live for something higher than the pleasures of our society or what the suburban church offers, who want to live for things of purpose and glory and honor. This means sacrifice and getting serious about holiness and forsaking self-centered living for others-oriented living. The good news is that we have a loving heavenly Father who is interested in those things. He wants the best for us, which means we cannot persist in immaturity. He will have a harvest of righteousness.

How, then, do we understand our trials and struggles? Instead of complaining, we must get on our knees and say, "Father, You love me. You have sent Your Son that I would be adopted as one of your children, and then You promised to care for me, and I have experienced that. You have dreams for me that I would scarcely dream for myself. I look forward to growing in grace, to being more holy, to being glorious! I look forward to my future history." God desires this for us because he is our Father. That is why he disciplines us.

The Privilege of Inheritance: Personal Promises from Our Heavenly Father

We have present blessings of adoption because we have access to "Abba, Father," such that we may come into God's presence in Jesus' name and be received by him. We also have his care, both in terms of spiritual care and circumstantial provision, and we have our Father's discipline. But the day will come when all who now are

sons and daughters of God in Jesus Christ will enter into
the glory of the full inheritance of God's children. In
the ancient world only sons inherited, which is why we
may rightly say that both male and female believers are
adopted into sonship with God. That is no fantasy or
science fiction but factual future history for the children
of God.

Paul puts it this way: we are co-heirs with Christ
(Romans 8:17). That does not mean that God chops up
eternal glory into pieces that everyone receives separately.
It means we inherit *all* of it *together* with Christ: we are
all *heirs together* of God's glory (Ephesians 1:5-6, 11-12;
3:6). What do we have to look forward to as Christians?
This is the question that adoption answers. We are heirs
of God's glory and all his goods; we will enter into
them eternally with Jesus. We will not experience all
the blessings of adoption in this life, but we have our
Father's promise that we will enter into his glory.

The Heart of Adoption

In adoption, God gives himself to us: He opens
our access to him and provides all that we need, even
when what we need is discipline. God does this for the
unlovely—those who were dead in sin and trespasses,
who were in bondage to the ways of Satan and the world
and sin, who were his enemies and justly under his wrath
(Ephesians 2:1-3). This is the cesspool out of which he
adopts us into his family in the Beloved, and he does this
by the redeeming blood of the Lord Jesus Christ.

Whatever stood between you and God, Jesus has

removed by grace, not because you stood out against the crowd in the great orphanage that is this world. There is no material to work with in us but demerit, guilt, and rebellion, but God says he wants to be glorified by taking the chief of sinners and making him glorious by grace. The truth about our relationship to God can empower us to live in light of his love. No longer must we live as servants, desperately trying to do something to win approval. Instead, let us live in glorious freedom as children of God.

A Modern Parable of Horizontal and Vertical Adoption

A couple in my church in Philadelphia wanted to have children because they had great love in their hearts from God. I ministered to them over three years in their intense struggle of childlessness, and they finally decided to adopt a child from Russia. They completed the legal work and one day received a photograph of a little boy. He had no idea, but there was suddenly a couple of Christians in America who began spending time with his picture. They gave him a name and started buying things for his room and praying for his whole life. So too, in eternity past, before the worlds were born, God knew his children and named them and poured out his love for them and planned all of what he would do in and through them before they even existed.

The day came when that couple got on a plane for Russia only to encounter many difficulties once they arrived. First, they received a scary medical report that turned out bogus. Then another family arrived from Eastern Europe and tried to take their child, resulting in a ten-day courtroom fight and unexpected expenses. Think too of the difficulties that God the Father came into this world to overcome so that you could be his child, primary of which was the problem of our guilt, which He overcame through the cross of Christ.

Human adoption is a picture of God's adopting love for us, but God's adoption of us can also teach us something about what it means to adopt human children. It is not easy, yet you have all you need if you are a child of God. Yes, you must love the child you adopted, but you have a great love *within you* because God has an eternal and everlasting and costly love *for you*. He gave what we could never imagine, sending his Son to die on the cross that he might love us. Will you then give your heart to God?

Give Me Your Heart

In Proverbs 23:26, God calls to us: "My son, give me your heart." Your heavenly Father wants your heart. Will you trust his Word? Will you live and feed off the promises of adoption? If you do, it will radically change how you look upon life and the world. You will marvel that you have received an inheritance in the beloved, and you will no longer seek your satisfaction in this world. Instead, you will have a new heart for the lost of the world.

Not everybody can adopt, nor is every Christian called to adopt a child, but the Church is called to look upon the world's lost. I know of no more beautiful expression of the gospel in our culture than for an unloved and maybe even unlovable child to be seen and loved by Christian families and Christian churches simply because of God's great love for them. That love is now within us, so we adopt that child and bring that child into our love. We raise that child in the knowledge of God in Jesus Christ. What more glorious, more wonderful thing can we do?

Adoption on a horizontal level is a picture of God's love for us, where God loves us and invites us to give him our hearts. But then he invites us to take his heart and look upon the lost, the alien, the fatherless, and bring them into his love. Believe God's Word that you have been declared God's dear sons and daughters, and walk in that truth, giving your hearts to him and receiving his heart as well so that you might live as his children in the world.

Six

THE FREEDOM OF ADOPTION

Scotty Smith

Of all the magnificent riches of the gospel, none is more to be treasured and pondered than our adoption in Christ. When the Father lavished his love upon us and made us his children, we weren't just street-wandering orphans looking for a good meal and a warm bed. We were self-absorbed slaves to sin and death. Indeed, we weren't in the orphanage of loneliness; we were in the morgue of hopelessness. Adoption, therefore, is the quintessential freedom for which we long, and for which we've been redeemed.

In essence, the Christian life is a lifelong journey of coming alive to the multifaceted freedoms we've been given as the beloved children of God. We begin the journey standing at the base of the Swiss Alps of the gospel, with a tiny spoon and a little sand bucket, trying to take it all in. But our joy lies in knowing the Father will bring to completion the good work he began in us, and in his whole creation.

It will take the second coming of Jesus for us to finally and fully "get" the utter wonder of our adoption. But until then, the Holy Spirit is powerfully at work in our hearts to increase our understanding and deepen our experience of the privileges and filial freedom of adoption.

The freedom of adoption can be understood from three perspectives: the freedom of legal rights, the freedom of personal delights, and the freedom of a missional life.

The Freedom of Legal Rights

Biblical adoption secures us in a state of objective blessings. As with our justification, so with our adoption, God generously gives us a stunning status that has absolutely nothing to do with our effort, deserving, or feelings.

The Legal Rights of Sons and Daughters

When God justifies us, many marvelous things happen. The very moment we are given faith to trust in Jesus, God declares that all of our sins, past, present, and future—sins of thought, word, and deed—are completely and eternally forgiven. The blood of Jesus doesn't just cover the four percent of our sin we're probably aware of, but also the other ninety-six percent about which we have no clue. Simultaneously with forgiving us, God also declares us to be righteous in his sight. He does this by imputing to us, or putting into our account, the perfect righteousness of Jesus. This is a legal, objective status which never wavers in intensity or degree. Once you are justified, you are 100 percent justified. On this glorious foundation, in this legal environment, adoption also comes to us as a forensic category, bringing with it many grand realities that are instantaneously ours.

In Galatians 4:4-7 Paul demonstrates how our adoption presupposes but is distinct from our justification in Christ. In fact, Paul seems to be making the case that our adoption is even more glorious than our justification, if such a thing can be imagined. God redeems us so that we might receive adoption. In this sense, justification secures and paves the way for adoption.

> But when the set time had fully come, God sent his Son, born of a woman, born under the law, to redeem those under the law, that we might receive adoption to sonship. Because you are his sons, God sent the Spirit of his Son into our hearts, the Spirit who calls out, "Abba, Father." So you are no longer a slave, but God's child; and since you are his child, God has made you also an heir.

This bit of rich theology comes to us as Paul was confronting a tragic situation in the province of Galatia. The churches in Galatia had "fallen from grace" — they became functionally disconnected from the beauty and power of the gospel. This was evidenced by their relational conflicts, their lapsing into a performance-based spirituality, and by a loss of joy among the believers. Paul used the doctrine of adoption in order to bring them to repentance.

In doing so, Paul was using the Roman economic and social construct of adoption and filling it with redemptive-historical meaning. Although Israel was declared to be God's son through adoption (see Hosea 11:1 and Romans 9:4), adoption was not a typical Jewish practice. But as with many themes in the history of redemption, adoption as a category emerges with greater clarity and prominence with the arrival of Jesus.

So when he wrote, "you are no longer a slave but a son," Paul had both Israel's redemption out of slavery and the Roman marketplace in mind—the environment where adoptions would take place on a daily basis. In Rome, someone who had the means could "redeem"— that is, buy a slave out of his bondage and legally make a slave into a son or daughter. Immediately, all the legal freedoms and privileges of being in the new family were conferred on the former slave. Paul drives this image home.

The Galatian Christians were behaving like they were common slaves, still in slavery to the unrelenting taskmaster of the law. Paul used the doctrine of adoption, along with its radical implications, to bring these joyless, divided believers back to "gospel sanity." To "lose" the gospel is to lose everything. Through the gift of Jesus, God did everything necessary to legally buy sinners out of their sin and debt.

By his life of perfect obedience, Jesus fulfilled the demands of the law for the children of God and, by his death on the cross, he exhausted God's judgment against their sin. Jesus became the ultimate slave to sin and death that we might become the legal and beloved children of God. It could be argued that an infinite overpayment was made to turn slaves into the beloved children of God. Paul's point? How could believers in Galatia mock the glory of their adoption by acting so immaturely, by acting like they aren't legally a part of the most glorious, graced-inundated family—the family of God? How can we?

The Legal Guarantee of an Inheritance

But there are still more legal benefits to consider. We're not just in God's family; we're in God's future and estate. In his opening remarks to believers in Colossae, Paul refers to God as "the Father, who has qualified you to share in the inheritance of the saints in the kingdom of life. For he has rescued us from the dominion of darkness and brought us into the Kingdom of the Son he loves."

Once again, notice the filial language here: God is presented as the Father who qualifies the unqualified to become his own sons and daughters. Next, the issue of family inheritance is introduced as a part of our adoption. Because we have been legally constituted sons and daughters of God, we have been made his legal heirs. For adopted children, inheritance is not a wage-earning category, but a grace-gift category.

So what kind of inheritance are we talking about? Everyone united by faith to Jesus, our elder Brother, will inherit the entire earth (Matthew 5:5)—that is, all the perfections and wonder of life in the new heaven and new earth (Revelation 21:1-22:6). How staggering! What measureless riches are ours in Jesus! The day is coming when all things will be united in Jesus, our elder Brother, "things in heaven and things on earth," for he is making all things new (Ephesians 1:10). Though we await acquisition of this inheritance, it is already legally ours (Ephesians 1:14).

The Legal Privilege of Discipline in Love

There's still more legal wonder to consider. Through our adoption in Christ, we make a legal shift from relating to God as our judge to relating to him as our Father who disciplines us in love. As we grow in grace, we emotionally transition from fearing God as a judge to surrendering to him as a loving Father. God intends for us to know him as Abba, Father, not Sugar, Daddy, for he is a father who disciplines (corrects) us, sometimes very severely, but always in love.

The writer of Hebrews presents this great truth in this way:

> Endure hardship as discipline; God is treating you as sons. For what son is not disciplined by his father? [8] If you are not disciplined (and everyone undergoes discipline), then you are illegitimate children and not true sons. [9] Moreover, we have all had human fathers who disciplined us and we respected them for it. How much more should we submit to the Father of our spirits and live! [10] Our fathers disciplined us for a little while as they thought best; but God

disciplines us for our good, that we may share in his holiness. [11] No discipline seems pleasant at the time, but painful. Later on, however, it produces a harvest of righteousness and peace for those who have been trained by it. (Hebrews 12:7-11)

The writer of Hebrews argues throughout his letter that Jesus is superior to Moses, angels, Aaron, Melchizedek, and everything that was written in the Old Testament. Everything in the history of redemption was given in anticipation of Jesus. Jesus is the "Yes" to every promise God has made. The shadow was intended to give way to the substance. And the excellence of Jesus puts us in a unique relationship with God as our Father.

To understand that Jesus suffered once and for all, for us, exhausting God's judgment against us for our sin, means that God will never deal with us according to our sins or reward us according to our iniquities. Because he has dealt with Jesus according to our sins, and rewarded Jesus according to our iniquities, now we have a Father who takes our sin so seriously and loves us so deeply that in his contra-conditional love, he will not give up on us. Even when his discipline is severe, we know that it is in love and that it yields the peaceable fruit of righteousness to those who are trained by it.

The Freedom of Personal Delights

The atoning work of the Son of God gives God's adopted children great freedom: we come alive to God's lavish love through a new legal status as adopted sons and daughters of the living God. But through adoption, we also receive personal delights that propel us forward into a missional way of life.

The Freedom to Delight in Subjective Wonder

Our objective status as adopted children should lead us to subjective (experiential) wonder, as we saturate ourselves and marinate in these great truths of how much God loves us. Our legal rights are intended to become personal delights. Adoption is not just a great doctrine to be intellectually understood as a part of good systematic theology. It's meant to rock our world, to move us to "palm up" adoration and worship of such a God who would love such a people like you and me. The objective reality of our adoption should generate within us an unspeakable joy—one that brings much glory to God.

Paul shows us what this looks like in Ephesians 3:14-19. In this text we discover how adoption brings us into a process of being re-parented by the only perfect Father. In the original Greek, the passage begins like this, "For this reason, I kneel before the Father, from whom all Fatherhood derives its name." Paul literally says that adoption is critical because there is only one Father who can deconstruct every earthly illusion about fatherhood. No human father can ever fill the Abba-shaped vacuum in our heart. And no human father can ever abuse, ignore, abandon, or wound us so badly that we cannot become alive and healthy through relationship with God as our

Father. There is only one perfect Father, and we get to know him only through the gospel of his grace.

Sigmund Freud said we created the notion of "father" and projected it upon God, but Paul says exactly the opposite, that the very category of "father" comes from God to us. Our heavenly Father is *the* Father from whom all Fatherhood derives its meaning. And this Father loves us so much that he has given us his only begotten Son to make us his adopted sons and daughters.

As Paul pondered the greatness of our Father and the glories of our adoption in Christ, he broke into a prayer in which he asked God to give us the power we need to experience the multi-dimensional love we have been given in Jesus—a love, Paul says, that is so great it surpasses knowledge. Even throughout eternity we will never exhaust our knowledge of God's love, and yet we are called to grow in our experience of this love on a daily basis. As we come alive to the Father who loves as no other father does, we are re-parented into that knowledge.

The Freedom to Delight in Gospel Transformation

Indeed, adoption grants us the freedom to come more and more alive to our Father's lavish love. But this is no mere selfish experience or religious high. God's love is a transforming love. Consider 1 John 3:1-3, where the apostle John positions himself like Paul, with astonishment, and bids us join in his astonishment:

See what kind of love the Father has given to us, that we should be called children of God; and so we are. The reason why the world does not know us is that it did not know him. Beloved, we are God's children now, and what we will be has not yet appeared; but we know that when he appears we shall be like him, because we shall see him as he is. Everyone who has this hope in him purifies himself, just as he is pure.

We must read these words with a certain degree of humble incredulity, because who could be more unlikely to be called the children of God but you and me? But that's just the point: we are declared to be God's children legally. It's something God has done for us in full view of our ill-deserving condition. But now, as we come alive to the radical implications of our adoption, we begin to live a whole new life. Such lavish love propels us into godly living. The indicatives of our adoption lead to the imperatives of transformation. Only the gospel gives us the motivation and power to please God from the heart—to offer our Father the obedience of faith and love. Only gospel astonishment will lead to gospel transformation.

The Freedom to Delight in Safe Vulnerability

Lastly, we consider a freedom that binds all these personal delights of adoption together: the freedom of never having to pose or pretend about anything before God. We are given the freedom of crying "Abba, Father" in our brokenness, our joy, our sadness, our suffering, our prodigality, our elder-brother self-righteousness. Christians are the only people on the planet who do not have to pretend about anything. We must savor this freedom as it is revealed in Romans 8:15-17:

> For you did not receive the spirit of slavery to fall back into fear, but you have received the Spirit of adoption as sons, by whom we cry, "Abba! Father!" The Spirit himself bears witness with our spirit that we are children of God, and if children, then heirs— heirs of God and fellow heirs with Christ, provided we suffer with him in order that we may also be glorified with him.

This word *Abba* is most closely related to the European title *Papa*. This unique word conveys the dignity of a respected father and the rich intimacy of *Dad*. As we experience the Spirit working in our hearts to give us the freedom to cry, "Abba, Father," we don't begin to relate to God as a celestial butler who has no real concern for the condition of our hearts—someone who exists simply to make us happy and comfortable. That wouldn't be love, would it? The cry "Abba, Father" reveals a deep awareness of his intimate love for you, an assurance that in every season of life, you enjoy the freedom to say, "Oh God, your mercy had better be a match for my heart, because right now I am a mess."

Even when we violate our peace with God through selfishness, we have freedom to cry out to him, to crawl into his lap, to be made whole. This is why we must continually preach the gospel to our hearts and to one another. Only in the assurance of God's love for us as Abba will we surrender all the chaos, weariness, brokenness, and longings of our hearts to him.

The Freedom of a Missional Life

We have contemplated two freedoms of adoption. First, the freedom of legal rights: adoption secures us in a state of objective blessings. Second, the freedom of personal delights: adoption calls us into a realm of subjective wonder. Now we consider, lastly, the freedom of a missional life: adoption propels us into the world with sacrificial hope.

We see this in Romans 8:18-25:

> For I consider that the sufferings of this present time are not worth comparing with the glory that is to be revealed to us. For the creation waits with eager longing for the revealing of the sons of God. For the creation was subjected to futility, not willingly, but because of him who subjected it, in hope that the creation itself will be set free from its bondage to corruption and obtain the freedom of the glory of the children of God. For we know that the whole creation has been groaning together in the pains of childbirth until now. And not only the creation, but we ourselves, who have the firstfruits of the Spirit, groan inwardly as we wait eagerly for adoption as sons, the redemption of our bodies. For in this hope

we were saved. Now hope that is seen is not hope. For who hopes for what he sees? But if we hope for what we do not see, we wait for it with patience.

Here, Paul applies the rich theology of adoption to how we live our lives, individually and corporately as the children of God. The more fully we come alive to the glory and grace of Jesus, the more deeply we understand and experience our adoption in Christ, and the more completely we will give ourselves over to a life of missional living and loving. The gospel produces sacrificial living because of its unparalleled giving.

To have the hope of final adoption is both a personal and cosmic reality. Not only in our hearts, but the whole creation is groaning for the Day when adoption in part gives way to the fullness of adoption. We are pregnant with glory!

Because the whole pan-national family of God will be adopted (just as God has promised), because Jesus is going to finish making all things new (just as he has promised), we can and must give ourselves over to offering this world the first fruits of the new heaven and new earth. This is why Christians should be the front-line lovers and servants in the world of human trafficking, poverty, hunger, injustice, and indeed, in the world of orphans. Because Jesus has signed on for eliminating the very category and word "orphan" from the human vocabulary, let's partner with him, one adoption at a time. We cannot fail. We cannot and will not possibly fail. Our labors in the Lord are, and never will be in vain!

Seven
ADOPTION AND MISSIONAL LIVING

Jason Kovacs

I remember the first time I walked into a church building and was struck by the number of families with adopted children. Even though I have multiple friends who were adopted, until that moment I had never seriously thought about adoption or the plight of the orphan. But there in the lobby were all these parents with children of different races. It was the first time adoption had been so visible to me. Clearly there was something different about this church. What was it?

Although new to the church, I soon began to realize these families were part of a much bigger group and a much bigger vision: to be a people who care passionately for the orphan. Over the years this church had developed a culture of adoption that had resulted in hundreds of children being placed in homes. It didn't matter who you asked in the church, adoptive family or not, they would tell you the same thing: We adopt and care for the orphan because God adopted us in Christ when we were without hope and home. The gospel was the motivation for what God was doing and continues to do in that congregation.

What I witnessed in this one church I am now witnessing in churches all around the country. But it is not a new thing. It is an expression of biblical mission and biblical compassion at work.

When we look at the Scriptures we find that adoption is far more than just child placement. Adoption actually rests at the very heart of the history of redemption. Biblically and historically it is the *foundation* and *goal* for the mission of the church to the world. In fact, it is impossible to read the Bible for long without encountering the deep concern God has for the fatherless. A pattern of justice and compassionate action towards the orphan starts with God himself, then Israel, Jesus, the disciples, and on to the early Church. The pattern has continued to this day, as the Church reflects God's heart for the poor and vulnerable.

The Gospel Leads to Mission

The natural result of a church or individual gripped by the saving grace of God in the gospel is a passion for taking that gospel to the world. As Lesslie Newbigin writes:

> Mission begins with a kind of explosion of joy. The news that the rejected and crucified Jesus is alive is

something that cannot possibly be suppressed. It must be told. Who could be silent about such a fact? The mission of the Church in the pages of the New Testament is like the fallout from a vast explosion, a radioactive fallout which is not lethal but life-giving.[41]

This mission includes not only the declaration of this good news but also the demonstration of it in our world. Mission is both declaring the words and works of Jesus and doing in the world what he has commanded us to do. It is the declaration that speaks the saving word. It is the demonstration that shows the living word. The church is the place where God's kingdom and his character are most manifest on earth. By doing justice the world is given a foretaste of the gospel and kingdom of God. Through the proclamation of the gospel the world is invited into the kingdom.

Adoption as Mission

Whatever your views are of mission and what it means to be "missional," it is hard to argue with the reality of Jesus' mission. He came to earth to live and die for the redemption and renewal of all creation. A central aspect of that redemption and renewal is the adoption of sons and daughters and the final consummation of creation in the finalization of their adoption (Romans 8).

Jesus is our best model for what missional living and the church's mission ought to look like. Missional Christians are to make disciples and to love their neighbors as themselves. One of the most powerful ways we can do this is through our care for the "least of these." Tim Keller points out: "God loves and defends those with the least economic and social power, and so should we. That is what it means to 'do justice'….From ancient times, the God of the Bible stood out from the gods of all other religions as a God on the side of the powerless, and of justice for the poor."[42]

God's power, mercy, and justice are most visible when they are unleashed for the sake of the weakest in our world, and few are weaker or more vulnerable than the orphan. Since the good news of the gospel is that when "we were still weak" (Romans 5:6) God came to us in Christ, orphan care provides us with a unique opportunity to model and demonstrate the kindness of God on the horizontal plane.

Biblically, adoption and orphan care are not primarily something we do because we are infertile or want to meet a great need. They are tangible demonstrations and pictures of the gospel—of God's adoption of us—put on display for the world to see and give glory to God.

Adoption and our care for the fatherless provide a visible demonstration of the gospel. Our adoption of children serves as a window into Christ's rescue of us. Adoption displays gospel-justice. Adoption displays the patient, persistent pursuit and sovereign choice of God for us. Adoption displays the heart of God for rescuing a people from every nation, tribe, and tongue. Because of what God has done for us in Christ, adoption and orphan care are signs that God's kingdom and rule are present in our world and will one day come in all their fullness.

The question, is what are our churches and our lives putting on display to our world right now?

Application

When I first walked into a church and noticed adoptive families all around me, it was because that church had embraced missional engagement with a strong emphasis on horizontal adoption. In other words, the gospel was increasingly affecting every part of their lives for the glory of God's grace in our fallen world, and it was impacting how they addressed the global orphan crisis. Undergirding this emphasis was a broad theological understanding of vertical adoption. Today, churches with this emphasis are much less rare than they used to be, but even so I am convinced God is calling a great many more churches to such an embrace.

The Church today has an unprecedented opportunity to make the gospel visible through caring for the orphan. Never in the history of the world have there been as many vulnerable and orphaned children in need of a family, or as many people in need of a Savior. What does it look like practically for the Church to care for the orphan as part of its gospel mission? Here is my encouragement for how churches can engage missionally with respect to horizontal adoption and orphan care.

The Church and the Orphan

Do not simply adopt orphan care as one ministry among many in the church. Integrate orphan care into the church's missional culture. Teach, train, and speak about the connection between our mission to the world and adoption. Create a culture that deeply values the fatherless because God does. An orphan-valuing culture will have a radical impact on the way a church conducts its orphan and adoption ministry both inside and outside its walls.

In this way, orphan care becomes much more than a ministry for a select few. The entire congregation takes ownership of it. The children's ministry is equipped and mobilized to care for adopted children. The small-group ministry is equipped to care for adoptive and foster families. The financial ministry has thought through the implications of adoption for a family's finances. The church budget reflects the heart of God for the fatherless.

A passion for adoption grown in the heart and mission of God will translate into a thousand different actions. Some church members will adopt. Some will foster. Some will finance adoptions. Some will pray and support families. Some will go overseas and give their lives to orphans and the gospel.

If you cannot move the culture of your church from the top down, be encouraged that many churches have had their cultures transformed by one couple or one person stepping out in radical, patient, and persistent faith. Often the example of one ordinary family or individual doing something that the world thinks is extraordinary is enough to tip the scale for a hundred others who are just waiting for something to happen.

As we seek to mobilize the Church with God's missionary heart that bursts to declare and demonstrate the gospel, the question will not be, "Who is called to care for the 'least of these'," but rather, "How might we care for them together?"

The Church and the City

Within our cities are hundreds or even thousands of orphans living in foster care and residential treatment centers. In the past these centers were called orphanages. Many people are shocked to hear there are still orphans in America. The reality is that there are more than 500,000 children in the U.S. foster care system. Roughly 130,000 of these have been legally deemed orphans and thus are available to be adopted. Sadly, most will not be adopted. Instead they will turn 18, age out of the foster care system, and disappear. These are the most fatherless of all, and among the most likely to perpetuate fatherlessness in the next generation.

This is where a church, motivated by vertical adoption and mobilized for horizontal adoption and orphan care, can step in and dramatically demonstrate the gospel to a watching world. Jeremiah says, "Multiply there [in the city], and do not decrease. But seek the welfare of the city where I have sent you into exile, and pray to the LORD on its behalf, for in its welfare you will find your welfare" (Jeremiah 29:6-7).

Is there any more tangible and visible way to care for the city than to care for its weakest and most vulnerable members? If the U.S. has 130,000 legal orphans, then this nation has more evangelical churches than it does waiting children. So the question is, in a country as wealthy as ours, why are there *any* waiting children?

At the very least, Jeremiah 29 calls churches to be actively praying to the Lord on behalf of their regions. Surely included in this are prayers for the fatherless, the social workers, the foster parents, and those involved in providing care for these children. By serving the city in this way a church has an incredible opportunity to meet a huge need that continually puts great pressure on the city, county, and state departments of Social Services. More importantly, a church has the opportunity to transform children's lives by providing them what they need most – a family, temporary or permanent, that will be committed to their welfare in every way possible, emotionally, physically, and spiritually. In all this, the church puts the gospel on vivid display.

To top all this off, there is the promise in this passage that in our pursuit of the good of these children in our city, we will find God caring for us. As we pour ourselves out and experience the pain, difficulty, and risk that comes with foster care and adoption, God will pour into us what we need.

What can be done?

Get together with other churches and evangelical leaders in your city and start a conversation about orphan care in light of God's gracious adoption of us. Some may already be making efforts in this area. Talk to your local department of social services and ask how you can help. Talk and preach about this subject until people see the wonder of vertical adoption and how it applies to horizontal adoption. Provide opportunities for people to step forward in faith to be a part of "seeking the welfare" of your city through foster care and adoption. And that is just a start.

God calls his people to seek the renewal of all things. Whether you call this missional living or simply Christianity, local churches should both recognize and act on the fact that it is not God's will for any child to be without a loving home and an opportunity to hear the gospel.

Is that your church?

The Church, Adoption, and the Nations

Along with the call to seek the welfare of our cities, the Church is called by God to make disciples of all nations. Missional living is not content with localized visions for the Church – there is an innate passion through the Spirit of God to see churches planted among every nation, tribe, and tongue.

Globally, more than 2.7 billion people are unreached with the gospel. Add that there are also roughly 163 million orphans globally, and we have a worldwide spiritual and physical crisis. The church on mission, as we have discussed, has a passion both to declare the gospel to all people and to demonstrate that gospel to all people.

We have a great calling and opportunity. The more I study it and the more I talk with those around the world who are doing both church planting and orphan care, the more I am convinced there is a biblical connection between the two and a crucial need to further flesh out

that connection. This is not a conversation many folks
are having – you don't hear the church-planting world
talking a lot about orphan care. And you don't hear the
orphan-care people talking about church planting. In
fact, I once heard from a major missions organization
that they discourage their church planters from engaging
in orphan care because it is a distraction to the mission
of the church. I think I understand what they mean
but I believe James, the brother of Jesus, would not let
that statement go unchallenged. If the practice of true
religion necessarily involves caring for orphans in their
affliction (James 1:27), then it seems to me that orphan
care must be an integral part of what a church is and does
missionally, no matter the size of the church. It is hard
to believe that the Great Commission and the call to
practice pure religion would be mutually exclusive.

Church Planting and the Orphan Crisis

God's passion is for his glory to fill the earth
(Habakkuk 2:14), to be seen and delighted in by people
from every nation, tribe, and tongue (Revelations 5:9ff).
The glory of God resides in and is spread through his
Church. His glory and gospel are spread as the Church
spreads (Ephesians 2:19-22, 3:7ff). The glory of God is
made known most clearly through the Church declaring
and demonstrating the gospel.

Therefore, we must be committed to church planting
and, to at least some degree, genuinely caring for the
"least of these." The Great Commission is a church-
planting commission. The great commandment—"You

shall love the Lord your God with all your heart and with all your soul and with all your strength and with all your mind, and your neighbor as yourself" (Luke 10:27) —is a compassion commandment(The greatest need for the orphan is for the Church to be the Church for them, declaring and demonstrating that the kingdom of God is at hand and is coming in fullness.)

While there are a lot of great organizations serving the orphan, only the Church has been divinely called by Jesus to do this work of making disciples and caring for the least of these. The Church holds our world's only hope for redemption and renewal. In fact, the Church *is* the new humanity, the literal foretaste of the heavenly city on earth. We know that in heaven there will be no orphans, and no orphanages, but only the family of God. God has empowered the Church with his Spirit and the power of the gospel literally to transform cities and nations. The gospel saves spiritual orphans and it transforms society for the sake of physical orphans. The Church is a family and is God's instrument to providing family to those who are without family.

Through church planting the gospel is taken into new places of need and the kingdom of God breaks further into dark places of need. With 2.7 billion people yet to be reached, and more than 40 million orphans among just the top 100 unreached people groups, the only church that can offer hope is a church willing to cross a culture.

How can we do this?

- Build a strong church-planting passion and orphan passion into the DNA of your church. It is estimated that 4,000 churches are planted each year in the U.S. alone. Imagine the impact if even a quarter of these churches had this DNA.
- Then commit to planting churches with similar DNA.
- Partner with the global Church to plant churches that declare and demonstrate the gospel. The U.S. Church alone is neither called to nor capable of caring for all the orphans of the world. If we are to make any lasting change it must be done through global partnerships between churches. We must aim for national movements of churches helping churches care for orphans.

Imagine if the Church took seriously the call to fill the earth with the glory of God through church planting—and those churches, planted among every nation, tribe and, tongue had a gospel-motivated passion for the fatherless. What a massive difference that would make.

Eight
ADOPTION: THE HEART OF THE GOSPEL

John Piper

The deepest and strongest foundation of adoption is located not in the act of humans adopting humans, but in God adopting humans. And this act is not part of his ordinary providence in the world; it is at the heart of the gospel. Galatians 4:4-5 is as central a gospel statement as there is: "But when the fullness of time had come, God sent forth his Son, born of woman, born under the law, to redeem those who were under the law, so that we might receive adoption as sons." God did not have to use the concept of adoption to explain how he saved us, or even how we become part of his family. He could have stayed with the language of new birth so that all his children were described as children by nature only (John 1:12-13, "But to all who did receive him, who believed in his name, he gave the right to become children of God, who were *born*, not of blood nor of the will of the flesh nor of the will of man, but of God."). But he chose to speak of us as *adopted* as well as being children by new *birth*. This is the most essential foundation of the practice of adoption.

Eight Similarities Between God's Adoption of Us and Our Adoption of Children

I pray that whether you have adopted, or assist with adoptions, or are pondering an adoption, God will use these comparisons to heighten your confidence that he is graciously involved in our adoptions. He has done it himself. He knows what it costs. And he stands ready to support us all the way to the end.

1. Adoption Was (for God) and Is (for Us) Costly

> When the fullness of time had come, God sent forth his Son, born of woman, born under the law, *to redeem* those who were under the law, so that we might receive adoption as sons. (Galatians 4:4-5)

To redeem means to obtain or to set free by paying a price. What was the price God paid for our liberation and adoption? "Christ *redeemed* us from the curse of the law by becoming a curse for us—for it is written, 'Cursed is everyone who is hanged on a tree'" (Galatians 3:13). It cost God the price of his Son's life.

There are huge costs in adopting children. Some are financial; some are emotional. There are costs in time and stress for the rest of your life. You never stop being a parent until you die. And the stresses of caring about adult children can be as great, or greater, than the stresses of caring for young children. There is something very deep and right about the embrace of this cost for the life of a child!

Few things bring me more satisfaction than seeing a culture of adoption flourish at our church, Bethlehem Baptist. It means our people are looking to their heavenly Father for their joy rather than rejecting the stress and cost of children in order to maximize their freedom and comforts. When people embrace the pain and joy of children rather than using abortion or birth control simply to keep children away, the worth of Christ shines more visibly. Adoption is as far as possible from the mindset that rejects children as an intrusion. Praise God for people ready to embrace the suffering—known and unknown (God's cost to adopt us was infinitely greater than any cost we will endure in adopting and raising children.)

2. Adoption Did (for God) and Does (for Us) Involve the Legal Status of the Child

> When the fullness of time had come, God sent forth his Son, born of woman, born under the law, to redeem those who were under the law, so that we might receive adoption as sons. And *because you are sons*, God has sent the Spirit of his Son into our hearts, crying, "Abba! Father!" (Galatians 4:4-6)

God had legal realities to deal with. His own justice and law demanded that, for our sins, we be punished and excluded from his presence. Righteousness was required and punishment demanded. God had to satisfy his justice and his law in order to adopt sinners into his family. This he did by the life, death, and resurrection of his Son, Jesus Christ.

This means that the status of *being* a son legally preceded the Spirit giving us the *joyful affections* of sons. The objective work of our salvation, 2000 years ago at Calvary, grounds the subjective experience of our salvation by the Spirit today.

So it is with our adoption of children: The legal transactions precede and undergird the growth of family feelings. If the legal red tape seems long and hard, keep in mind that this tape is not yet red with your blood—but Jesus satisfied all the legal demands precisely by shedding his blood.

3. Adoption Was Blessed and Is Blessed with God's Pouring Out a Spirit of Sonship

Because you are sons, God has sent the Spirit of his Son into our hearts, crying, "Abba! Father!" (Galatians 4:6)

You did not receive the spirit of slavery to fall back into fear, but you have received *the Spirit of adoption as sons, by whom we cry, "Abba! Father!"* The Spirit himself bears witness with our spirit that we are children of God. (Romans 8:15-16)

God does not leave us as aliens when he adopts us. He does not leave us without feelings of acceptance and love. Rather, he pours his Spirit into our hearts to give us the experience of being embraced in the family.

What is remarkable about these two texts is the term, *Abba*. It is an Aramaic word. Why then does Paul use it, transliterated, in these two letters written in Greek? The answer is that it was the way Jesus spoke to his Father, in spite of the fact that virtually no one in Jewish culture referred to God in this endearing way. Jesus' use of the term stunned the disciples, and they held onto it as a precious remnant of the very voice of Jesus in the language he spoke.

In adopting us, God gives us the very Spirit of his Son and grants us to feel the affections of belonging to the very family of God. In his mercy, God also works in our families to awaken in adopted children affections for their parents that are far more than legal alignment. These are deeply personal and spiritual bonds. Adopted children do not *infer* they are our children by checking out the adoption papers. A spirit pervades our relationship that bears witness to this reality. Like the other children in the family, they all cry, "Daddy."

Praise God that he gives us *both* legal standing as his children *and* the very Spirit of his Son so that we find ourselves saying from a heart of deep conviction, "Abba, Father."

4. Adoption Was (for God) and Is (for Us) Marked by Moral Transformation through the Spirit

> All who are *led by the Spirit of God* are sons of God."
> (Romans 8:14)

To be led by the Spirit of God as a son of God is to think and act in accordance with the will of God, something we could never do on our own. But God does not leave us, his adopted children, without help to bear the moral image of the family; he sends his Spirit to lead us.

We may trust, also, that God's help will be there for our own children as we bring them under the means of grace that God uses to awaken and transform his children.

5. Adoption Brought Us, and Brings Our Children, the Rights of Being Heirs of the Father

> Because you are sons, God has sent the Spirit of his Son into our hearts, crying, "Abba! Father!" So you are no longer a slave, but a son, and if a son, then *an heir through God*. (Galatians 4:6-7)

The Spirit himself bears witness with our spirit that we are children of God, and if children, *then heirs—heirs of God and fellow heirs with Christ*, provided we suffer with him in order that we may also *be glorified with him*. (Romans 8:16-17)

In Galatians 4 (heirs "through God"), the context is the promise of Abraham. Our inheritance is *through* God because God, in sending his Son to redeem us, made us heirs with Abraham. Even though many of us are Gentiles, our adopted sonship makes us heirs with Abraham of the *world* (Romans 4:13).

In Romans 8 (heirs "of God"), the context is that we, with Christ, are heirs of all that God has—namely, everything. "All things are yours, whether Paul or Apollos or Cephas or the world or life or death or the present or the future—all are yours, and you are Christ's, and Christ is God's" (1 Corinthians 3:21).

Just before we left for England on a sabbatical, Noël and I went to a lawyer and updated our wills. All our boys are married and Talitha, our adopted daughter, is the only legal "dependent." A lot had changed since we had made our wills. This was a reminder to us that Talitha will inherit like the sons. She does not hold some lesser status because she is adopted. All inherit together. That is the way God did it. That is the way we do it.

6. Adoption Was (for God) and Is (for Us) Seriously Planned

> He chose us in him before the foundation of the world, that we should be holy and blameless before him. In love *he predestined us for adoption* as sons through Jesus Christ, according to the purpose of his will, to the praise of his glorious grace, with which he has blessed us in the Beloved. (Ephesians 1:4-6)

Adoption was not Plan B in God's mind. There was no Plan A with lots of children who never sin and never need to be redeemed. God predestined us for adoption before the creation of the world. Plan A was creation, fall, redemption, adoption so that the full range of God's glory and mercy and grace could be known by his adopted children. Adoption was not second best. It was planned from the beginning.

In our lives, there is something uniquely precious about having children by birth. That is a good plan. There is also something different, but also uniquely precious, about adopting children. Each has its own uniqueness. Your choice to adopt children may be sequentially second. But it does not have to be *secondary*. It can be as precious and significant as having children by birth. God is able to make adoption an A+ plan in our lives.

7. Adoption Was (for God) and Often Is Now (for Us) from Very Bad Situations

> We . . . were by nature *children of wrath*, like the rest of mankind. (Ephesians 2:3)

God did not find us like an abandoned foundling bundled on the front step and irresistibly cute. He found us ugly and evil and rebellious. We were not attractive. We would not be easy children to deal with. And, what's worse, God himself was angry with us. He hates sin and rebellion. We were then doubly "children of wrath."

These are the ones God pursued in adoption.

Therefore, all of God's adoptions crossed a greater moral and cultural divide than any of our adoptions could. The distance between what we are, and what God is, is infinitely greater than any distance between us and a child we might adopt. God crossed the greatest cultural barrier to redeem and adopt us.

Consider too, that according to Romans 9:4, the people that God chose in the Old Testament, the Israelites, were adopted out of a terrible situation. "*They are Israelites, and to them belong the adoption*, the glory, the covenants, the giving of the law, the worship, and the promises." But how was this adoption effected? Hosea 11:1, "When Israel was a child, I loved him, and *out of Egypt I called my son*." They were slaves in Egypt. But not only that, they were often also rebellious against God. "Our fathers, when they were in Egypt, did not consider your wondrous works; they did not remember the abundance of your steadfast love, but rebelled by the sea, at the Red Sea" (Psalm 106:7).

Therefore, God went and took a son from Egypt who was both enslaved and rebellious. The pattern is set: adoptions do not just come from nice, healthy, safe, auspicious situations.

8. Adoption Meant (for All Christians) and Means (for Christian Parents) that We Suffer Now and Experience Glory Later

The whole creation has been groaning together in the pains of childbirth until now. And not only the creation, but we ourselves, who have the firstfruits

of the Spirit, *groan inwardly as we wait eagerly*
for adoption as sons, the redemption of our bodies.
(Romans 8:22-23)

Why does Paul say we are "waiting for our
adoption"? Aren't we adopted already? Yes, when
Christ died for us, the price was paid, and when we trust
him, we are legally and permanently in the family. But
God's purpose for adoption is not to leave any of his
children in a state of groaning and suffering. He raised
Jesus from the dead with a new body, and he promises
that part of our adoption will be a new resurrection
body with no more disabilities and no more groaning.
Therefore, what we wait for is the *full experience* of our
adoption—the resurrection of our bodies.

There is much groaning in the path of adoption on
the way to full salvation. But the outcome is glorious.
It is worth it all. "I consider that the sufferings of this
present time are not worth comparing with the glory
that is to be revealed to us" (Romans 8:18).

This is especially relevant for parents of children with
disabilities. They know the "groaning" of this life. All of
us have children with some sort of disability, and some
of us will live to get very old and watch our children
age and die before we do. Others will see their children
struck down in war or by accident or disease. Others will
care for a disabled child till one of them dies. All of this
groaning is groaning in hope because we are adopted by
God and destined for a resurrection and an eternal future
of health and wholeness and joy. It will be worth it all.

Adopting Talitha Ruth

In conclusion, it might be helpful for you to know some of the process that Noël and I walked through in deciding to adopt Talitha. We spent long hours and days in 1995 pondering and praying over whether to adopt. It was not a light or easy decision. I was fifty years old. Here is the letter I wrote to Noël saying *yes*.

Monday, November 6, 1995, 11:12 PM

Dear Noël,

With confidence in the all-sufficient future grace of God, I am ready and eager to move ahead with the adoption of Talitha Ruth. I want to thank you that during these years, when your heart has yearned to adopt a daughter, you have not badgered me or coerced me. You have been wonderfully patient. You have modeled faith in the sufficiency of prayer. You have always expressed support of me and my ministry even if we should never adopt. You have been reasonable in all our discussions and have come forth with your rationale only when asked. You have honored my misgivings as worthy of serious consideration. God was good to put it in Phoebe's heart to call about this child when she did, and not before we were ready.

I realize more than ever that "the mind of man plans his way, but the Lord directs his steps." This decision is not merely a tabulation of pros and cons. I would be deceiving myself to think that. Yet I am persuaded that this decision to adopt honors God more than not adopting. To my perspective, it seems to be the path that will "spread a passion for the supremacy of God in all things for the joy of all peoples." I believe it will bless Bethlehem and not hinder our work there. I believe it is the path of the greatest love for the greatest number. And therefore I have confidence that God is pleased with it.

I choose it not under constraint or with any reservation of commitment. I relinquish every thought that, because you initiated this idea, you will bear blame for the burdens it will bring. As with our choice to have children in the first place and with our choice to go to Germany and our choice to leave Bethel and enter the pastorate, there is a common and united commitment to all that God will be for us in this path, including any "frowning providence" that he plans to sanctify to us. I believe our eyes are open, though we have learned that the toothache expected and the toothache experienced are not the same. We have come through enough to believe that God's future grace will be sufficient. His mercies are new every morning and there will be mercies for every weight and wonder on this new path of our lives.

I thank God for you. I enter with you gladly on this path. Whether we live to see our daughter grown or not, we will have done well to take her in. Life is very short, whether 12 hours like Ashley Hope, or 50 years like me, or 76 years like my father, or 94 years like Crystal Anderson. What matters is not that we do all we might have done or all we dreamed of doing, but that, while we live, we live by faith in future grace and walk in the path of love. The times are in God's hands, not ours.

With this common conviction, we will, God willing, embrace our new daughter and give ourselves, with all the might that God inspires in us, to love her into the kingdom. May the Lord establish the plans of our hearts, and bring Talitha Ruth (and the future husband God already knows) into deep and lasting fellowship with Christ. May she be an ebony broach of beauty around your aging neck and a crown of purity and joy on your graying head.

I love you,
Johnny

Editor's Acknowledgments

Thanks to my wife, children, and parents for loving me unconditionally.

Thanks to Downtown Presbyterian Church for making much of the gospel.

Thanks to Drs. Timothy Trumper and David Gardner for radically shaping my thinking on theological adoption.

Thanks to Kevin Meath, Jennifer Strange, and Johnston Moore for pouring over these pages.

Eternal thanks to my Abba Father and to Jesus, the greatest older Brother anyone could ever have or want.

About the Authors

Dan Cruver and his wife, Melissa, are parents of a multi-ethnic family of three children. Dan is the director of Together for Adoption, an organization that provides gospel-centered resources to mobilize the church for global orphan care. Dan is a frequent conference speaker and writer. He has a M.S. in Counseling and 90+ hours toward a Ph.D. in Theology. Prior to directing Together for Adoption, Dan was a college professor of Bible and Theology and a Pastor of Family Ministries.

John Piper is the Pastor for Preaching at Bethlehem Baptist Church in Minneapolis, Minnesota. He grew up in Greenville, South Carolina, and studied at Wheaton College, where he first sensed God's call to enter the ministry. John is the author of more than 30 books and more than 25 years of his preaching and teaching is available free at desiringGod.org. John and his wife, Noël, have four sons, one daughter, and an increasing number of grandchildren.

Scotty Smith is Founding Pastor of Christ Community Church in Franklin, Tenessee and a Council member with The Gospel Coalition. Scotty has written five books: *Unveiled Hope*, with Michael Card; *Speechless*, with Steven Curtis Chapman; *Objects of His Affection*; *The Reign of Grace*; and *Restoring Broken Things*, with Steven Curtis Chapman.

Richard D. Phillips is Senior Minister of Second Presbyterian Church in Greenville, South Carolina. God has called him to a writing ministry and he regularly authors books and articles. Among his twenty-one books, his most recent include a commentary on Zechariah, *Jesus the Evangelist*, and most recently *What's So Great About the Doctrines of Grace*.

Jason Kovacs is the Director of Ministry Development for The ABBA Fund, a ministry that provides financial resources to Christian couples and churches to help make adoption possible. He also serves on staff as Pastor of Care and Counseling at the Austin Stone Community Church. He and his wife live in Austin, Texas with their five children (four adopted and one biological child). Prior to the ABBA Fund, Jason served as a director of a biblical counseling center and as a pastor in Charlotte and Minneapolis.

ENDNOTES

1. Timothy Keller, *The Prodigal God: Finding Your Place at the Table*; www.Redeemer.com.
2. C.S. Lewis, *The Weight of Glory* (Harper One, 2001) p 42
3. The occurrences of "adoption" in Paul's writing's can easily be arranged chronologically along the timeline of the story of redemption (e.g., Ephesians 1:4-5; Romans 9:4; Galatians 4:4-5; and Romans 8:15, 23). Dr. Timothy Trumper fleshes this out wonderfully in "A Fresh Exposition of Adoption I. An Outline," in Scottish Bulletin of Evangelical Theology 23 (2005) pp 60-80. No one has helped me more in this understanding of Paul's use of "adoption" than Trumper.
4. By "triune," I mean that God is Trinity. Wayne Grudem defines the Trinity as follows: "God eternally exists as three persons, Father Son, and Holy Spirit, and each person is fully God, and there is one God" (*Systematic Theology: An Introduction to Biblical Doctrine*, p 226).
5. Sinclair B. Ferguson, *Children of the Living God* (Banner of Truth, 1989) p 27
6. Tim Keller, *Counterfeit Gods: The Empty Promises of Money, Sex, and Power, and the Only Hope That Matters* (Dutton, 2009) xiv
7. Ibid. xvii
8. Cornelius Plantinga, *Not the Way It's Supposed to Be: A Breviary of Sin* (Wm. B. Eerdmans Publishing, 1995) p 131
9. *The Confessions of St. Augustine: Modern English Version* (Paraclete Press, 1995) pp 15-16
10. George MacDonald, *Proving the Unseen* (Keats Publishing, Inc.) p 67
11. George MacDonald, *A Dish of Orts; Chiefly Papers on the Imagination, and on Shakespeare* (Forgotten Books, 2010) p 103
12. *Proving the Unseen* (Keats Publishing, Inc.) p 72
13. To play off the words of Genesis 1:1 and John 1:1.
14. Dr. Douglas Kelly, in his Systematic Theology I lectures at Reformed Theological Seminary, addressed this very question. My comments here are based upon the portion of his lecture on the Trinity that addressed this issue.
15. Kevin Vanhoozer, *The Drama of Doctrine: A Canonical, Linguistic Approach to Christian Theology* (Westminster John Knox Press, 2005) p 53

16. Thomas F. Torrance, *The Christian Doctrine of God: One Being Three Persons* (T & T Clark International, 2001) p 220

17. Douglas Kelly, *Systematic Theology, Vol. 1* (Mentor, 2008) p 407

18. "The Plural pronoun, 'Let us make man', suggests a God who is plural and communal. God creates through his word and now that word is addressed to himself. God is personal and he exists in community. What constitutes the image of God in man is a much-debated issue, but it seems that one element of what it means to be God's image bearers is this communal nature. The God who said 'Let us' makes us relational beings. We are people in community. He did not make us solitary. We are made male and female. We are made to exist in community and we are made for community with God. The Trinitarian community graciously extends its communal life" (Tim Chester, *From Creation to New Creation* [Paternoster Press, 2005] p 42).

19. Dave Gibbons, *The Monkey and the Fish: Liquid Leadership for Third Culture Leader* (Zondervan, 2009) p 82

20. *The Christian Doctrine of God: One Being Three Persons* (T & T Clark International, 2001) p 165

21. *Ibid.* p 207

22. *The Monkey and the Fish: Liquid Leadership for Third Culture Leader* (Zondervan, 2009) p 82.

23. Thomas F Torrance, *Ground and Grammar of Theology: Consonance Between Theology and Science* (T & T Clark International, 2005) p 155.

24. Cited in McGrath, *Thomas F. Torrance: An Intellectual Biography* (T & T Clark International, 2006) p 74

25. A paraphrase of this Torrance quotation: "God is not one thing in himself and another thing in Jesus Christ" (*The Christian Doctrine of God*, p 243).

26. *Systematic Theology, Vol. 1* (Mentor, 2008) p 556

27. The Greek text only has "son" the first time: "the son of Joseph" (Luke 3:23). Even though it is absent throughout the remainder of the genealogy, it is implied in each case.

28. *Children of the Living God*, pp 6-7. The full quotation: "How important is sonship in biblical teaching? We can express its centrality abruptly but truly by saying: Our sonship to God is the apex of creation and the goal of redemption. God's first man was created as his image in order to be his son. Luke suggests that Adam was 'the son of God' in his genealogy of the Lord Jesus Christ (Lk. 3:38). To be a son, in the language

of Genesis, was to be made in the image and likeness of one's father. So, when Seth was born to Adam and Eve, the event is recorded in these terms: 'When Adam had lived 130 years, he has a son in his own likeness, in his own image' (Gen. 5:3). Exactly the same phrase is used about the relationship between God and Adam. God made man in his image and likeness (Gen. 1:26-27; 5:1-2). To be a son, and to be the image and likeness of your father, are synonymous ideas. To put it another way, if we wish to understand what man was intended to be, we need to think of him as a son of God."

29. Cited in Timothy Keller, *Counterfeit Gods* (Dutton, 2009) ix

30. Timothy Keller, *The Prodigal God* (Dutton, 2008) p 37

31. James Torrance, "The Vicarious Humanity of Christ" in *The Incarnation: Ecumenical Studies in the Nicene-Constantinopolitan Creed A.D. 381*, ed. Thomas F. Torrance (Handsel Press, 1981) p 141

32. John Calvin, "Psychopannychia," *Tracts & Treatises in Defense of the Reformed Faith, III*, p 454, cited in Calvin's Ladder: A Spiritual Theology of Ascent and Ascension (Eerdmans, 2010) p 83

33. Thomas F. Torrance, *Atonement: The Person and Work of Christ* (IVP Academic, 2009) p 151

34. Michael P.V. Barrett, *Complete in Him: A Guide to Understanding and Enjoying the Gospel* (Ambassador-Emerald International) pp 166-167

35. Herman N. Ridderbos, *Paul: An Outline of His Theology* (Eerdmans, 1997) p 59

36. Ibid. p 108

37. Romans 3:24; 6:11, 23; 8:1, 2, 39; 9:1; 12:5; 15:17; 16:3, 7, 9, 10; 1 Corinthians 1:2, 4, 30; 3:1; 4:10, 15, 17; 15:18-19; 22, 31; 16:24; 2 Corinthians 1:21; 2:14, 17; 5:17; 12:2, 19; Galatians 1:22; 2:4, 16-17; 3:14, 26, 28; 5:6; Ephesians 1:1, 3, 9, 12, 20; 2:6, 7, 10, 13; 3:6, 11, 21; 4:32; Philippians 1:1; 2:1, 5; 3:14; 4:7, 19, 21; Colossians 1:2, 28; 1 Thessalonians 2:14, 16; 5:18; 1 Timothy 1:14; 3:13; 2 Timothy 1:1, 9, 13; 2:1, 10; 3:12; Philemon 8, 20, 23; Hebrews 3:14; 1 Peter 3:16; 5:10, 14

38. Ephesians 1:4, 7, 10, 11, 13; 2:15, 22; 3:12; 4:21

39. Calvin's *Institutes*, II.12.3

40. C.S. Lewis, The Weight of Glory (MacMillan, 1962) pp 4-5

41. Lesslie Newbigin, The Gospel in a Pluralist Society (Eerdmans, 1989) p 116

42. Timothy Keller, *Generous Justice: How God's Grace Makes Us Just* (Dutton, 2010) pp 5-6

Wrestling with an Angel

A Story of Love, Disability, and the Lessons of Grace

by Greg Lucas

"C.S. Lewis wrote that he paradoxically loved *The Lord of the Rings* because it 'broke his heart' – and Greg Lucas' writing does the same for me."

Justin Taylor
Managing Editor
ESV Study Bible

"Witty... stunning... striking... humorous and heartfelt. In our culture which is so quick to devalue life, *Wrestling with an Angel* provides a fresh, honest look at one father's struggle to embrace God in the midst of his son's disability. Can sheer laughter and weeping gracefully coexist in a world of so much affliction? Greg knows all about it. And inside these pages he passes on his lessons of grace to us. I highly recommend this wonderfully personal book!"

Joni Eareckson Tada, Joni and Friends International Disability Center

"You will laugh; you will cry. You will feel sick; you will feel inspired. You will be repulsed by the ugliness of sin; you will be overwhelmed by the love of God. Greg Lucas takes us on an unforgettable ride as he extracts the most beautiful insights into grace from the most painful experiences of life."

David P. Murray, Puritan Reformed Theological Seminary

"This is not primarily a book for parents of special-needs children. There is only one disability that keeps a person from heaven, the sin that lives in our hearts. Greg Lucas is a captivating storyteller. When he writes about life with Jake, I recognize God's grace and loving persistence in my life. I want more!"

Noël Piper, Author, and wife of pastor and author John Piper

CruciformPress

- We release a new book the first of each month.
- Our books are all essentially the same length.
- They are all exactly the same price.
- We intend each one to be clear, inspiring, helpful, well-written, attractive, and theologically reliable.

SUBSCRIPTIONS
Print $6.49
Ebook $3.99

Choose from ePub (for iPad, Nook, and many other e-readers), Mobipocket (for Kindle), or PDF.

Subscriptions are charged monthly. You save money and a short, helpful, high-quality, gospel-focused book arrives every month. Our website and newsletter (plus Twitter and Facebook) will keep you posted on what books are coming next. You can cancel at any time simply by emailing us. www.CruciformPress.com/Subscriptions

BULK PRINT SALES, ANY TITLE
6 to 50 books $7.45
51 books or more $6.45

www.CruciformPress.com/Our-Books

KINDLE OR iPAD

Order our ebooks by name directly
from your Kindle or iPad $5.99

Made in the USA
Lexington, KY
30 December 2010